# From Betrayal Trauma to Healing & Joy

*A Workbook for Partners of Sex Addicts*

# MARSHA MEANS, MA
COAUTHOR OF YOUR SEXUALLY ADDICTED SPOUSE

A Circle of Joy
Healing for lives touched
by sexual addiction

"A Neuro-Theology of Sex and Addiction," a DVD by Darrell Brazell (newhopeforsi.com), transcribed and quoted in Chapter 7 is used with permission of Darrel Brazell.

Copyright © 2011, 2014, 2017, 2020 by Marsha Means, MA

All rights reserved. No portion of this book may be reproduced or transmitted in any form whatsoever, including electronic, mechanical or any information storage or retrieval system, except as may be expressly permitted in the 1976 Copyright Act or in writing from the publisher. Requests for permission should be addressed to: marsha@acircleofjoy.com.

Editorial and design services by Keith and Sarah Fletcher Hanan Communications (hananhouse.com)

Means, Marsha
From Betrayal Trauma to Healing & Joy: A Workbook for Partners of Sex Addicts (Fourth Edition, Rev. 1)

ISBN: 9781654271039

A Circle of Joy Press

Printed in the United States of America

# Contents

Introduction .................................................................................................. vii
Guidelines for Sharing .................................................................................. ix
Wisdom from The Word ............................................................................... xi
Pathways to Healing..................................................................................... xii
Turning Points for Growth ............................................................................ xv
1 – The Tasks & Tools for the Journey Ahead ............................................... 1
2 – Handling & Processing Your Emotions ................................................. 13
3 – Personal Empowerment & the Art of Detachment ................................ 27
4 – Self-Care & Self-Soothing for Empowerment: Part I ............................ 45
5 – Boundaries ............................................................................................. 63
      Boundaries: Part II ............................................................................... 73
6 – Lost & Found: Finding Treasures in Your Trauma Chest ..................... 83
7 – Finding Your Way Back to You ............................................................. 91
8 – Looking Ahead: Forgiveness, Trust & Beginning Again ..................... 109

## Appendices

Appendix A: How We Can Increase Our Capacity So We Can Heal .......... 123
Appendix B: Understanding What It Means to be Male, Wounded & Addicted ... 127
Appendix C: When Your Marriage Fails.................................................... 143

# Introduction

If you have purchased this workbook, or joined a support group that uses it, you have probably been hurt by your partner's sexual betrayal. The pain that comes from emotional or physical betrayal is almost indescribable for most women. Research shows that 69% of us experience trauma upon discovering our husband's betrayal, and many develop post-traumatic stress disorder (PTSD) when their trauma continues, unhealed, over time. Healing is essential.

To begin to heal, you need several things. You need time and a process to help you work though the betrayal and focus on taking care of yourself. You need safe people to talk to, people who truly understand and care about what you are feeling; and you need to know you won't be judged. A support group made up of women who are going through similar experiences provides the appropriate setting. Each of our husbands have betrayed their vows in some way, and our common pain produces empathy between us.

But the support group must commit to hold confidential any information you share so that you can feel safe when you open your heart. An important part of feeling safe in a group is the bond that grows between you and the other women. For this bond to develop, it's important that you make the group sessions a priority in your life as you work through the workbook's process. You need to work hard to attend each session, unless there is an important reason to be absent. And you need to let your group facilitator know ahead of time if you must miss. That way the others in the group won't worry about you, which we always do, because we grow to care deeply about one another.

Participation in such a group isn't dependent on how your husband has acted out sexually; what matters most is the deep, searing pain you feel. As partners of these men, our lives have been turned upside down, and to heal, we have a journey of our own to take. This workbook provides the first leg of that journey.

Many women have walked this path before you, and many have found healing. May "the God of all comfort" heal your heart in the weeks ahead.

Your sister on this journey,

*Marsha Means*, MA

P.S. The principles in *From Betrayal Trauma to Healing and Joy* are an elaboration of those found in *Your Sexually Addicted Spouse: How Partners Can Cope and Heal*, which I wrote with Barbara Steffens, PhD. I encourage you to use it for the suggested supplemental reading assignments given in some of the workbook chapters so you gain the much needed foundational pieces for your individual recovery and the group process ahead of you.

# Note From The Author

I'm so sorry you need this book, because that means your heart is broken and you likely feel alone in your pain. But bravo for searching for resources and help. I've been there, so I know how betrayal shreds our hearts, and it's something none of us were prepared for. My team and I are available to you for a FREE hour-long call. It's our gift for every new woman who comes our way, with absolutely no strings attached, because we remember how desperately we needed support and direction when we were where you, now, find yourself. We would love to hear your story, answer your questions, and tell you about free resources.


With your healing at heart,

Marsha Means, MA


FREE one-hour call at   www.BetrayalTraumaToHealingAndJoy.com

# Guidelines for Sharing

1. For people to feel safe sharing openly and deeply, there must be an agreement among all members to keep group members' identities confidential.

2. Be careful not to interrupt when others share, or ask them questions without asking for and receiving their permission first. Don't make negative comments on, or evaluate what someone else has said. And be especially careful not to give advice. Called "cross-talk," these things eliminate the feeling of safety to share whatever is on your heart, knowing you won't be judged, and no one will try to "fix" you. Safety is what makes a group work.

3. However, as you bond with the other group members, you will find that a more relaxed give-and-take develops between you, and as it does, the "rules" will relax a bit. Remembering to respect and honor our differences is key to safety, along with holding in high regard the boundaries of others in the group.

4. If you would like feedback from someone else in the group, you can ask for it. If you are asked to give another woman feedback, share out of your own experience using "I" statements, rather than giving advice.

5. If this is a therapist-led group, the therapist will undoubtedly ask questions or make comments that she thinks might be helpful in your healing and growth, though she should not give advice. While questions help a therapist help you, always remember that you are in charge of your boundaries, and "No" is a perfectly acceptable answer.

6. As you share, be sensitive to the time so everyone has the opportunity to talk. If you lose track of the time, the group facilitator may need to gently remind you. Please try not to feel embarrassed if that happens. All of us tend to forget the time when we are grieving and sharing it with others. That's just part of being human.

7. And lastly, some helpful tips for groups facilitated over the telephone:

Be careful not to breathe into the mouthpiece of your phone. Occasionally someone does this without realizing it and it's very loud on the receiving end. Secondly, if you have a dog that barks, or a baby that cries, or there is noise in the room you are in, please use the mute button on your phone when you aren't actually talking. It's a nuisance for you, but it enables the others on the call to hear you and the others share. Also, using an earpiece often creates static on the conference call line, as can using speaker phone or having a second phone near the phone you're talking on. Occasionally the conference call technology will drop a caller, or someone may have difficulty logging on to the call. These are annoyances, but generally, if you try again you'll make it in to stay. Though imperfect, these lines enable us to connect with each other across vast space so we can heal together.

## NOTE ABOUT ANSWERING QUESTIONS IN THIS WORKBOOK:

Please write in longhand your responses to the many questions in this workbook. As you do, and as you share them with each other in the supportive group environment, you participate in moving your pain along the pain processing pathway in your brain. Doing this helps "metabolize" your experiences and your feelings. So, pick up a pen and fill the lines provided throughout the workbook. Search deep within for your own authentic answers. We have also provided blank pages at the end of this workbook for additional therapeutic writing and doodling.

# Wisdom from The Word

## Key Biblical Principles Upon Which the Group Is Based

Over and over in Scripture, God emphasizes the importance of telling the truth.

- In Ephesians 4:15, Paul exhorts us to "speak the truth in love."
- In Psalm 32:3, David says "When I kept silent, my bones wasted away all day long."

It's no wonder that Jesus said, "You shall know the truth, and the truth shall set you free." The following two keys unlock and open the doors to emotional, spiritual, and relational health: (1) learning and understanding the truth about the circumstances of our lives and our reality, and (2) having the courage to share our reality with other people who are safe so the painful parts of our stories can be processed.

When we decide not to share important parts of our reality with anyone, we are making a decision to keep parts of our lives a secret. When we feel pain, but choose to keep it a secret, the power of that pain increases inside us. When we are able to share our secrets in a format that leads to healing, the pain decreases and is eventually integrated into our life story. This is why Scripture tells us in Ecclesiastes 4:1, "I saw the tears of the oppressed–and they have no comforter. . . ," and in Galatians 6:2, "Carry each other's burdens, and in this way you will fulfill the law of Christ."

My prayer for you is that during the weeks ahead this group will become a safe place to share your reality, including the secrets that are now breaking your heart.

## A NOTE ABOUT SEXUAL BEHAVIOR AND THE LAW

If part of your husband's behavior involves violating children in any way, including child pornography, the law requires this information must be reported to the appropriate officials. If this is true of your case, and you share that information in group, please know that is one piece of information that cannot legally be kept confidential. If you find yourself in this painful situation, I encourage you to report it to Child Protective Services yourself immediately. Though incredibly difficult, this is very important in order to protect your rights and responsibilities to your children. There have been cases when choosing not to report has resulted in the innocent parent also losing custody of her children. That's a consequence no child should ever have to live through, and more than most mothers' hearts can bear.

# Pathways to Healing

| Stages of Healing | Resources and Techniques for Stages of Healing |
|---|---|
| • Initial Discovery and Crises | • Find initial support immediately<br>• Reestablish safety<br>• Increase Capacity<br>• Consider controlled, supportive environments for disclosure; consider including polygraph testing<br>• Get tested for sexually transmitted diseases<br>• Practice good self-care<br>• Gain Self-Awareness |
| • Find/Build Good Support System<br>• Reestablish Safety (continued) | • Family and/or friends if "safe"<br>• Clergy if "safe"<br>• Counselor-sex addiction and trauma specialist, if possible<br>• "Partners of Sex Addicts" support groups<br>• Doctor's or psychiatrist's help if you're struggling with depression or anxiety. *If you feel suicidal, seek help immediately!* |
| • Create the Boundaries You Need to Feel Safe in Your Home Again | • Do you need sexual boundaries with your partner?<br>• Do you need a temporary separation from your partner: in-home or geographically?<br>• What other boundaries do you need? |
| • Practice Good Self-care in Each Area | • Mental/emotional self-care<br>• Physical self-care<br>• Spiritual self-care |
| • Create Boundaries Between Yourself and the Trauma | • Use self-care to build a boundary from the pain<br>• Learn and utilize self-soothing techniques<br>• Eliminate cognitive distortions<br>• Eliminate negative self-talk<br>• Use healthy self-talk |
| • Counter Dissociation if it is a Problem | • Use grounding techniques to stay present<br>• Use healthy self-talk to counter cognitive distortion that can lead to dissociation<br>• Use your impersonal energy to access your strength and stay in the present |

| Stages of Healing | Resources and Techniques for Stages of Healing |
|---|---|
| • Begin Emotional Processing and Grieving | • Recognize and process your feelings<br>• Acknowledge and grieve your losses and the consequences they produced in your life<br>• For some, face and adapt to separation or divorce<br>• Alter your attachment to what you've lost by letting it go and saying goodbye<br>• Develop resiliency |
| • Use Grieving and Processing Methods to Help Heal | • Externalize the problem by sharing your story<br>• Renegotiate the trauma with a counselor's help<br>• Consider nature-based healing or expressive therapy such as art or music therapy if talk therapy doesn't meet your needs<br>• Consider body therapies if talk therapy fails to bring healing and/or when trauma manifests in physical symptoms<br>• Consider EMDR if talk therapy fails to bring healing and/or when trauma manifests in<br>• physical symptoms |
| • Continue Emotional Processing | • You will know when the pain has lost its power and you are free to let it go and move on |
| • Develop Personal Empowerment | • Continue and expand healthy boundaries<br>• Develop solid grounding<br>• Strengthen your self-awareness<br>• Strengthen your impersonal energy/executive awareness<br>• Develop healthy communication skills<br>• Develop healthy conflict management skills<br>• Reframe yourself as a survivor rather than a victim |
| • Integration and Transformation Resulting in Post-Traumatic Growth | • Integrate the trauma into your life story<br>• Consider forgiveness<br>• Find new hope by transforming the pain into a positive life purpose. |

*From Betrayal Trauma to Healing & Joy*

# Turning Points for Growth

...recovery from rape is a grief process

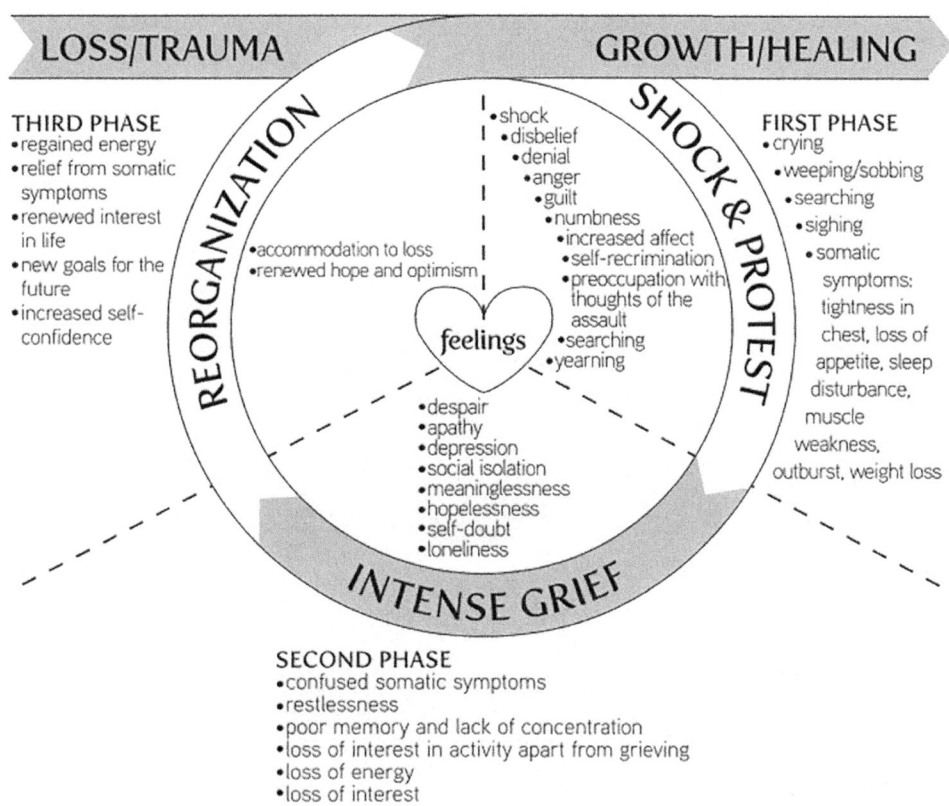

This chart is included in your *Journey to Healing & Joy* workbook as a way to compare what and how you feel to the way rape victims feel following being raped. As you look at the chart, starting at the top and moving clockwise around the wheel, can you identify with the feelings and symptoms listed here? Does it strike you as interesting—or perhaps horrifying—that you are experiencing the same feelings and symptoms a rape victim would?

Strangely, no one questions whether or not a rape victim feels trauma and post traumatic stress, unless they want to blame her for the rape. However, many still question whether or not partners of sexual addicts experience trauma or post traumatic stress disorder. And most go further still and label you as codependent, and somehow at least partially responsible for the catastrophe in your marriage and in your life as a result of your husband's addiction.

*From Betrayal Trauma to Healing & Joy*

Does seeing this chart help you to know you are not crazy for feeling the way you do? We hope it will give you permission to take good of care of you over the next several months, treating yourself gently and lovingly, just as you would do for a sister or a daughter whom you learned had been recently raped. The best way for you to avoid complications of post traumatic stress disorder (PTSD) in the years ahead is to slow down now and give your mind, body, and spirit what they require now in order heal during this season of heartache in your life. Try not to grow impatient with yourself. Many professionals say healing from this heartache can take three to five years, but from my personal experience, I know you can heal much faster if you make doing the work your priority now.

*Marsha Means, MA*

# 1

# The Tasks & Tools for the Journey Ahead

**Helpful Supplemental Material if You Have Time:**

- Read Chapter 3 of *Your Sexually Addicted Spouse: How Partners Can Cope and Heal*
- Listen to *Brain Science of Sex and Addiction* and *Attachment* by recovering sex addict, and pastor, Darrell Brazell, at http://newhope4si.com/audio/.

## The Trauma of Partner Betrayal

I know that if you need this workbook, your story, dreams, and plans for the future have been shattered by partner betrayal trauma. You gave your partner your heart, body and soul, and the key to your most-innermost parts, and he crushed them. And whether your marriage has ended, or you are still living together as a couple, you have lost something precious because of your partner's sexual betrayal. Most of us feel that we've lost many things, at least temporarily.

The emotional, physical, and spiritual attachments a couple shares create a deep bond, and when that bond is broken, the loss results in incredible pain. A host of overwhelming and unpredictable emotions leave us feeling powerless to manage our lives. We experience a loss of emotional safety and the loss of personal empowerment to protect ourselves and our children from further hurt. And we feel as if we don't know the man who shares our bed.

Relationship trauma—betrayal trauma—is the most piercing kind of emotional pain humans can experience. And without help and guidance, it's virtually impossible to heal. When I was where you now find yourself, I remember thinking I would surely die in my sleep because the almost unbearable crushing weight of the losses this betrayal brought with it were more than I thought my body and mind could bear. Yet I survived, and so can you. But please take care of yourself, because you are the only one who can.

## How Ongoing Trauma Can Become PTSD & Even Damage Your Health

Often women's' relational trauma recurs because the sexual acting out continues, or new, dribbled-out disclosures continue to be revealed, generating fresh waves of pain. And when that happens, not only is healing interrupted, but the reestablishment of the safety required to begin to heal is once again broken, throwing us back to the beginning of the healing process. With recurrence comes intensified trauma that can set up a cycle of post-traumatic stress disorder in our lives. And when trauma becomes PTSD, it becomes more complex and harder to heal.

Have you experienced recurrences of trauma when your husband acted out again, or disclosed new things that weren't revealed during his first disclosure? If so, what has that been like for you? In Chapter Two we'll help you gain the understanding and empowerment necessary to confront this cycle and ask that it stops, so you can heal, and hopefully protect your health.

_____

_____

_____

_____

## Trauma & Your Physical Health

"When the natural healing process is interrupted, the pain can intensify and become chronic," says trauma expert, Tana Slay, Ph.D. "The chronic nature of trauma pain can develop into severe emotional disorders." We also know emotional trauma can foster physical health problems.

When you're traumatized, no matter what the cause, your brain cycles and recycles the details of the traumatic event, trying to make sense out of something that is nonsensical. This keeps the brain on hyper-alert, which in turn dumps neurochemicals into your bloodstream. As excess neurochemicals bathe our cells, the inflammatory response is set in motion, and slowly, unhealed, long-term trauma takes a toll on your health and well-being.

French-American Pulitzer Prize winner Rene Dubois wrote, "What happens in the mind of man is always reflected in the disease of the body." We've seen that truth reflected in the lives of women again and again as we talk with them and hear their stories.

Have you experienced changes in your physical health that you attribute to this trauma in your life? If so, what are they?

_____

_____

_____

_____

We want to do everything possible to help you prevent lifelong health complications as a result of your husband's betrayal. So we urge you to prioritize your healing, and to determine what changes you need to make healing possible, then take action to make those things a reality.

## Trauma & Depression

Many partners who have experienced sexual betrayal struggle with severe depression. Stress can lower the brain's level of neurotransmitters, leaving you mired in dark, emotional sludge, unable to cope or feel joy in your life. If you feel depressed, look ahead to chapter 2 of this workbook, and read about HeartMath; then try the exercise at the link in that section of the chapter. This exercise has become central to managing my own emotions, and I'm hoping it will be helpful for you too. But if ultimately, you are stuck in depression, you may need a doctor's help. Hopefully you and your doctor can find natural ways to relieve your depression. But if nothing natural works, know that in the end, many of us need antidepressant medication to help us get through this chapter of our lives. I did, as do many millions of others. It's hard to be a great mom when we're depressed, and it can be impossible to heal trauma when the dark cloud of depression never lifts.

## Trauma & Anxiety

Some women experience intense anxiety or panic attacks after discovering their husbands' sexual behaviors, leaving them emotionally paralyzed. These important warning signs are telling us it's time to take extra steps so our bodies—including our brains—can calm enough to begin to heal. If you experience anxiety, discuss this with your doctor and find ways to remove as much stress as possible from your life. I've found the HeartMath exercise is hugely beneficial with anxiety too, but if it doesn't work for you, seek other medical help. Psychiatrists are the medical doctor's who are best trained to prescribe medications for complications of trauma, if it is needed.

Have you experienced depression and/or anxiety or panic attacks since discovering betrayal trauma in your marriage? If so, how are you dealing with them?

_____
_____
_____
_____

## STD Testing

None of us, especially when married, want to ask a doctor for an STD test. We feel humiliated and afraid of being judged, but being tested is essential. Your life could depend on it. Many among us discover we have a sexually transmitted disease, even if our husbands deny physical contact with someone else. In truth, few among us gain access to the whole truth about his sexual activities without a polygraph test.

So be your own best friend and take this proactive step; your life may depend on it.

## How Great Is Your Emotional Capacity?

Karl Lehman, MD, a psychiatrist and trauma specialist, uses the term, "capacity," when he writes and speaks about how to heal from trauma. But what does that word have to do with our emotional pain? Let me explain.

When an engineer designs a bridge, he knows the capacity of the bridge must to be at least as great as the possible number of vehicles that can be on that bridge at any one time. Otherwise, the bridge will collapse under the weight of too many vehicles, and people will fall to their death.

When Dr. Lehman talks about capacity, it's in reference to how much *emotional* pain we can carry before we collapse, and possibly plunge to our death. Our capacity—our ability to hold up under the weight of our emotional distress—*must be greater than the emotional pain we are carrying, or we cannot heal.*[1]

How great is your capacity right now? Do you think you have the emotional strength to bear up under the emotional pain betrayal trauma has produced in you—and find your way to healing on your own?

_____

_____

_____

Over the many years I've done this work, I've learned that few of us, including myself, have great enough "capacity" to find our way to healing the excruciating pain betrayal trauma produces without taking steps to increase our capacity. It's simply more than we can carry on our own. However, *we can increase our capacity through life-giving, joy-producing relationships with other safe women who understand our pain.*

Dr. Lehman's diagram, The Pain Processing Pathway, on the opposite page, helps explain how relationships fit into the picture of healing our trauma.

In this intentionally over-simplified diagram, Dr. Lehman reflects the beginning of healing from trauma with the word **PAIN.** He then uses an arrow to indicate how processing the pain to healing requires five essential components before our traumatic experience fills the "cup of our life" with knowledge, skills, empathy, wisdom and maturity. The five components include:

1) Maintain organized attachment
2) Stay connected

---

[1] Karl Lehman, MD, *The Immanuel Approach for Emotional Healing & Life*, (Evanston, Il: Immanuel Publishing, 2016), page 37.

3) Stay relational
4) Navigate the situation in a satisfying way, and
5) Correctly interpret the meaning of what's happened in our relationship.

Dr. Lehman teaches that if we can manage all five steps, we will heal with no long-term damage from the trauma.

However, steps 1, 2, and 3 *all require other people—safe, supportive people.* Recovery is a team sport. We simply cannot do it solo. To heal well, we need safe, supportive relationships, as reflected in Dr. Lehman's diagram. Relationships that produce joy, because our trusted support

## The Pain Processing Pathway2

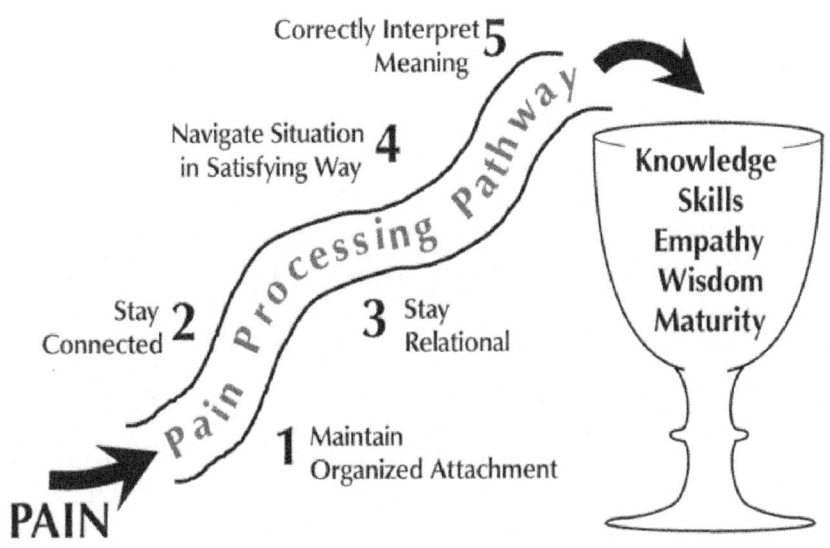

[1]Lehman, Dr. Karl, M.D., *Outsmarting Yourself: Catching Your Past Invading the Present and What to Do about It*, (LIbertyville, IL: This JOY! Books, 2011), 5.

people know about our pain, but they stay connected and love us through it. And steps 4 and 5 require a knowledgeable guide to help us navigate our way through our trauma so that in time, this part of our story becomes just another chapter in our life history, devoid of negative energy. We need each other. For this reason, I hope you are working through this workbook with a facilitated support group, led by a woman who has enough healing to guide you through a healing process in a safe, supportive group.

---

[2] Karl Lehman, MD, *The Immanuel Approach for Emotional Healing & Life*, (Evanston, Il: Immanuel Publishing, 2016), page 38.

*From Betrayal Trauma to Healing & Joy*

## The Power of the Group

Knowing this, as we begin this healing journey together, the greatest gift we can give (and receive) from one another is safety, empathic listening, and supportive encouragement. Studies reveal that we heal best when we have people in our lives who know our full story, but are still "happy to be with us"—people who will listen without judging—even if we hurt. That kind of safety grows attachment bonds, which produce joy, and these joy-bonds actually become one of our tools for healing. As a group, we need to commit to being present for one another, and for ourselves, during our time as a group, unless there's a good reason to miss sessions.

But for a few, staying connected proves challenging, and they isolate instead of connecting. When this happens, healing is stymied. I occasionally see this pattern interfere with a group member's healing, and the reason is nearly always rooted in her childhood. If you struggle to bond with other safe women, please read Appendix A to gain more understanding of this impediment, and what it takes to overcome it. You are worth the work required to heal well.

## The Role Safety Plays in Our Healing

To heal from the trauma we experience when a partner betrays us, we need to reestablish safety in our lives. In this context, the word *safe* doesn't mean "safe that he won't hit you, or harm you physically." It simply means the at-ease, comfort-of-home-safety we generally feel in our own space. Learning that betrayal is a part of our marriages can shatter that kind of safety, if we still share a home with our husband; particularly if he has entertained other sexual partners there.

If we don't feel safe, it is essential that we find a way to make home feel safe again. For some women, this may mean asking their husband to sleep in a different room for a while. Others find they need their husbands to live elsewhere for a period of time. Some turn a guest room or office into their own private retreat, and use it for privacy and self-care and sleep. And still others feel safe keeping things the way they are. Each of us is different; there is no right or wrong way to gain safety. The important thing is listening to your body and spirit and giving yourself what you need to begin to heal.

Our needs and circumstances vary, but one thing remains true for all: we must do whatever it takes to restore a sense of safety in our environment so we can relax enough to begin healing the trauma that betrayal brought into our lives.

Do you feel safe—meaning comfortable and relaxed—in your home and bedroom right now? Or do you need to initiate changes in order to sort things out, relax, and begin your healing journey? Why or why not?

_____
_____
_____
_____
_____

If you don't feel safe, what can you do to create the safety needed to "return to calm" so your heart, mind, and body can heal from the impact of betrayal and its resulting trauma? If you need guidance on how to ask for what you need, we will discuss this topic further in chapter 2.

_____
_____
_____
_____
_____

If changes are needed, how and when can you begin to make these changes?

_____
_____
_____
_____

## Giving Ourselves Grace

Early in discovery, most of us struggle to cope with everyday life. I lost, dropped, or broke nearly everything I touched for the first several weeks after disclosure. And my memory all but disappeared. How I wish I had known this gem back then, which I later learned from a working, single mother of six:

*"All I can do, is all I can do. And all I can do is enough."*

That's the sound of giving yourself grace, and grace plus time and space for healing are all essential. Grace is also self-care. Grace is giving yourself permission to let some things go. Without making room for our own recovery, we cannot heal well.

Are your feelings about your husband's behavior interfering with your ability to carry out your responsibilities? If so, in what ways? If your trauma is interfering with your daily functioning, how might you give yourself grace to make room for the time, space, and energy healing requires?

___

## Develop Keen Self-Awareness

An important part of early trauma recovery includes developing a keen sense of self-awareness. Self-awareness means we stay in touch with our bodies, minds and emotions throughout each day. It means regularly asking ourselves, "What do I need right now?" As women we tend to focus on caring for others and often overlook the necessity of caring for ourselves as well. But after experiencing trauma, coming to know what we need moment by moment is crucial to our healing. Giving ourselves breaks and making connections that create joy is absolutely essential. What is your greatest current need, and how might you get that need met?

___

## The Role Faith Can Play in Our Healing

A few pages ago I quoted Dr. Lehman as saying, *"We have been created to be relational beings—we have been created to be in relationship with God and with each other."* I know for some of us God is a painful subject, or something we think may not think even exist. For others, "God" has been used as a tool of abuse. If you fall into one of these groups, I challenge you to consider "a power greater than yourself." The sex addicts in our lives are learning to do that in their 12 step Sex Addicts Anonymous groups, because beating addiction on their own is virtually impossible.

But so is healing from trauma. Believing in a power greater than ourselves who is an unseen guest in every moment of our lives can greatly augment our capacity. You won't share this journaling question and answer out loud in the group; it is only for your personal, private processing. If you don't yet have faith in a power greater than yourself, how might using your imagination to test God's viability augment your capacity? And if you do have faith in a power greater than, how does your relationship with God augment your capacity?

_____
_____
_____
_____
_____
_____
_____
_____
_____

One of the first tasks in our healing journey involves facing and accepting reality. For those who have felt this betrayal, facing reality means coming to a place where we are willing to accept that this *really* has happened in our most intimate relationship. Until we face this reality and *accept* it, we usually stay mired in a mix of reeling emotions that trap us in circular thinking and anxiety, and we can't begin to heal. Have you reached that place of acceptance? The willingness that says, "This is my reality, whether I like it or not. It is what it is. Now what can I do about it?"

If not, how might you make room for, or cultivate a desire to, accept your present reality? Can your faith help you move toward accepting this as your reality so you begin to heal? If so, how? If not, what might help you move toward acceptance?

_____
_____
_____
_____
_____
_____
_____
_____
_____

## Change

Change is painful, especially when we didn't invite it. We prefer the familiar; we give it value—even if it hurts—because it's what we know.

We avoid change when we ignore what our *gut* is telling us. We deny what we know in our bones. We ignore intuition; we pass by insight. We hold on, afraid to change a pattern, even when it causes deep pain.

Change throws us into a period of transition. We feel conflict, pain, tension, fear, confusion. Our feelings signal us that change is trying to happen. Don't avoid it or withdraw. Don't turn to busyness or denial. Lean into the feelings; make space for them. Work with the necessary changes. Take the risk. It's all part of facing, accepting, and moving slowly toward the healing going on inside you.

As time passes, and as you recognize, experience, and express each emotion, your pain will finally begin to ease. Eventually, you'll be able to function normally again, although you will view many aspects of life quite differently. But this process can take many months, and for some, a few years. If you still struggle to heal after working through this workbook with a guide, please participate in an ongoing group such as ISA (isurvivors.org) or Celebrate Recovery. Connections provide a crucial element in your eventual healing.

## Tasks, Tools & Truths Discussed in this Chapter

1. Understanding trauma, PTSD, and the impact on our health
2. The need for STD testing
3. The Pain Processing Pathway explanation
4. Increasing your capacity through life-giving connection and support
5. Beginning self-care by using internal boundaries while sharing and listening to stories
6. Increasing "safety" at home by determining and asking for what you need
7. Giving yourself grace during this healing process
8. Developing keen self-awareness to know what you need
9. Considering faith to augment your capacity
10. Preparing for change and finding acceptance of your current reality

## APPLICATION: APPLYING TRUTH TO LIFE

From my work in this section I realize that I need to take the following action steps:

_____
_____
_____
_____
_____
_____
_____
_____
_____
_____

# 2

# Handling & Processing Your Emotions

### Helpful Supplemental Material if You Have Time

- Read pages 105–126 of *Your Sexually Addicted Spouse*. Pay special attention to the top two squares of the chart on page 109, as they help you recognize where you are in your healing process and what steps will help you heal.
- Read Chapter 5 of *Your Sexually Addicted Spouse*, especially if you are experiencing symptoms of PTSD and other health complications of trauma.

If, until now, you haven't had safe people to talk to about what's going on in your life, you likely feel as if you've been holding a huge ball under water, trying to keep it from popping up. The pressure of holding down so much pain and mixed emotion is almost unbearable. Even with people to talk to, you may feel as if you're drowning in the reality you now know is your life.

Putting feelings into words gives them shape and meaning, and gets them out of our heads. When our feelings stay trapped in our heads, they tend to repeatedly cycle, causing circular thinking, or what we term "an endless loop." When we get stuck in that conveyor-belt brain pattern, it's hard to determine what we need or want to do, and it becomes very difficult to make decisions. It also becomes impossible to heal.

Yet, simply talking about our feelings isn't enough, as we learned from Dr. Lehman in chapter one. We need support and joy-producing connections with others to increase our emotional capacity, and a guide and a forward-moving process, so we can face our pain and process it.

As you connect at a heart level and form attachments to the other women in your group, you will begin to want to keep your *relational circuits* on with each other and stay connected, even in between sessions. As you grow those connections with each other, your group time and space will become a place where you can live Steps 1, 2, and 3 in Dr. Lehman's diagram in Chapter 1. The group becomes a safe place to share your story, your pain, and begin to heal because you are now with safe women who understand, and who grow to love and care about you.

*From Betrayal Trauma to Healing & Joy*

## Two New Tools to Help You Do the Work in this Chapter

Before we dive into doing more healing work that involves processing pain, I want to equip you with two new tools that will help you do good self-care as you read and do this work. Please use each of these tools so you can process *and* do good self-care, because self-care is another one of our tools for healing.

## Creating Grieving Containers

For most of us, our emotions, including fear and grief, may be so pervasive they control our every waking moment, leaving us powerless to live life normally, and interfering with sleep. The concept of grieving containers provides one way to try to "manage" our emotions so we can do the things life requires of us, even as we grieve and work through feelings. I learned firsthand the value of creating grieving containers when my father, whom I loved dearly, died. I was in my last semester of earning my Master's degree in Marriage and Family Therapy. Interestingly, I was taking a grief and loss class *when my father died,* which meant I was studying how to help future clients face what I then faced.

Simultaneously I was overwhelmed with the need to grieve—to be alone, curled up my sofa at home with a blanket, where I could let myself feel and grieve my loss. However, my university did not allow for absences. Period.

Fortunately, the course text and our able instructor introduced us to the concept of grieving containers. I learned this concept means choosing periods of time, and/or certain places in our lives where we will give ourselves permission to intentionally grieve. Giving ourselves our own private time-out from life creates "parentheses"—space—for mourning. But they also leave room to keep *doing* life when we must. They break the times of grieving into smaller, shorter periods of time, giving us a way to conceptually manage our emotions.

I chose my morning shower, the commute to and from school, and the commute to my internship job. And though it was hard, it worked. I couldn't pack my general sadness away; it was simply too pervasive, so there were tears in public. But I was able to make it to class and work every day, with the exception of time out for the funeral, without stuffing my feelings.

Have you ever used your own form of grieving containers? If so, did they help you grieve adequately while doing life? How might grieving containers benefit you right now as you process your trauma while trying to function in life?

_____
_____
_____
_____
_____

## HeartMath Exercise

Recently I made a wonderful discovery called HeartMath. As a result, a simple exercise I've learned from them has become my favorite tool for managing my emotions. While I want to briefly introduce it to you here, you can read more about it in my e-book, *You Can Beat Anxiety Without Meds*. And HeartMath provides a wealth of free information on their packed website, heartmath.com, including a free, down-loadable e-book.

HeartMath is a nonprofit, scientific organization that's been doing research on the interaction between our brains and our hearts for nearly 30 years. Their study has led to scientifically proving that we can synchronize our brain rhythm and heart rhythm by using a simple appreciation exercise. It's an exercise we can do for ourselves; it only takes a minute or two, and it's absolutely free. But for those whose trauma is extreme, like war veterans, they've developed two pieces of technology that will maximize your efforts to bring what they call "coherence" between your brain and your heart, and with coherence comes calm. Please take five minutes and watch a brief video at heartmath.com/science. You will be so very glad you did.

On their website you can also find a video in which two war veteran's share how their lives have been radically changed by their use of HeartMath technology that augments the appreciation exercise for those with extreme PTSD. I promise you it will touch your heart and give you hope.

And to help us do the HeartMath appreciation exercise without a technological device, they've created a colorful, simple exercise tool you can print and use. You will find it at:

https://www.heartmath.org/resources/heartmath-tools/heartmath-appreciation-tool-and-exercises/

My hope is that you will do this exercise at least three times during the day so "coherence" becomes your new normal, even now, early in your healing journey. And that it will help you as much as it is helping me as I currently navigate a different, but difficult time in my own life.

## Identifying & Sorting Our Emotions

Because our emotions seem to have themes, it can be helpful to sort them into piles, the way we sort laundry. Sorting them makes them easier to manage and work through. Some emotions pertain to our relationship with the one who betrayed us. Some pertain to our loss of "safety." Others represent fears, like loss of our health and income. Several relate to feeling emotionally safe, and others link back to our past. Let's begin with those that involve our committed relationship.

## Facing the Reality of Marriage in the Digital Age

Because the integrity of our marriage relationship has been broken, each of us has lost at least two illusions: (1) We are so special to our partners that they would never betray us; and (2) The intimacy we shared with our husbands would last a lifetime without being violated. Both are enormous losses, and force us to rethink our vision of marriage.

If you're like most women, no one told you that many men—including Christian men—fight a lifelong battle with lust and sexual temptation. Fairy tales and romantic movies taught us that marriage vows would never be broken, even in a man's head. Discovering those stories are only childhood myths shatters our dreams and our belief system. And they require a new understanding of the way the male brain works. Appendix B shares the neuroscience of sex addiction and the male brain, and is helpful in understanding the reality of marriage, especially in the digital age, if you haven't already read it elsewhere. Let's talk about that new reality.

What were your assumptions about your marriage and future on your wedding day, and how has your view changed?

_____
_____
_____
_____
_____
_____
_____

Some of us are totally blindsided by this discovery, and some, like one group member said she did, "Paint all the red flags green." I realize that I, too, did that. Did you ignore, put up with, cover up, or spiritualize *(i.e., "God will take care of it.")* your husband's behavior in any way, because you didn't know how to deal with it? If so, how?

_____
_____
_____
_____

No matter how you answered that last question, what is helping you face the truth now?

_____
_____
_____
_____

The losses relating to our marriage relationship and the losses related to safety intersect and have bearing on each other, *because it is the one you love that has left you feeling unsafe.* It gets further tangled because many women want comfort from the man they love—but it's the one they love who hurt them! And that creates emotional dissonance, like clashing music in a song.

Trust is gone, and so too is safety. Some seek comfort by being sexual with their betrayer, only to end up feeling used. A support group can be enormously helpful when our emotions are so confusing. The group (and the support between sessions) provides a safe place to share, ask for input, and consider what we need or want to do to get our needs met in a healthy, healing way.

## Safety Losses Due to Triggers

In chapter one, we talked about safety in the bedroom, but the loss of safety can be far more reaching than life at home. Suddenly, restaurants, malls, the kids ball games and practices, grocery shopping—and even church—are triggers because young, head-turning women are everywhere. And they often dress to maximize their youth and beauty. Many women find going anywhere with their husband is simply more than they can bear in the beginning, because they don't have sufficient healing to face fresh waves of pain, nor do they yet have all the tools to help with this kind of triggering.

Where are you in regards to being with your husband in public? Do you find that triggering situations interrupt your safety and disrupt your healing at this juncture? How can you best take care of yourself in regards to triggers at this point in your healing?

_____
_____
_____
_____
_____
_____

In chapter three we'll learn to use the tool of detachment, which is enormously helpful and enables us to better care for ourselves in a world full of triggers. And we'll spend two weeks on boundaries later on. Each of these tools will help empower you to tackle these challenging topics.

But for right now, what do you need to feel safe with your husband? Or maybe to feel safe *without your husband for a while?* Remember, there is no right or wrong answer to any of these questions; there is only the correct answer for you and where you are right now.

_____
_____
_____
_____

If your husband is *still* acting out, I strongly suggest you seek one-on-one counseling, in addition to your group, to get the focused help you need. There can be no safety while living with a sex addict who is still in his addiction. But for some, this presents an Everest-sized challenge. Young moms who stay home with their children, and older women who are at least partially economically dependent on their husbands are the women who face the greatest challenges in creating safety in their homes and lives, because their options are limited. But with the help of a counselor who understands these challenges, you can put together a long-term plan, and begin to work toward it. If its needed, I suggest you skip ahead and read the Detachment and Boundaries chapters. Reading them now can help you understand the roles these skills play in your self-care, as you face your husband's continued sexual betrayal.

Do you currently need to confront your husband about anything, or ask him to make changes to help make room for your healing? If you aren't certain, remember that we'll gain a lot of new skills and strengths in future chapters. Our goal is to give you what you need to help you begin to heal now, while continuing to equip you in the weeks ahead.

*However, if he is still acting out and you want to confront him and ask for change, doing this in a way that works usually requires outside help. A counselor trained in sex addiction might be helpful. Or friends or family members who understand the addiction and what's happening in your lives can help. Both the Mayo Clinic and the Betty Ford Foundation offer helpful information online, explaining how interventions work. But do seek advice if you are in this uncomfortable place right now. Living with ongoing betrayal is terribly hard on your health.*

_____
_____
_____
_____
_____

# Losses That Hook the Past

## *Abandonment*

As I wrote a few pages ago, some of our losses hook our history, especially our childhood history. And generally, the more trauma childhood held, the stronger our reaction to our current betrayal trauma. If we experienced abandonment in childhood, our husband's betrayal can hook that earlier abandonment. Do you feel any abandonment because of what he's done? Why or why not?

_____
_____
_____
_____
_____

Have you experienced feelings of abandonment, or actual abandonment, at other times in your life? If so, does the current situation bring up old pain? For some of us, the two kinds of abandonment get so tangled together it becomes difficult to determine which one we're responding to. On the positive side, having the past come up again creates another opportunity to heal old wounds. What's going on inside you related to feelings of abandonment?

_____
_____
_____
_____

## *"Don't Talk Rules" in Childhood*

Another way our new betrayal trauma can intersect with our childhood trauma comes in the form of "don't talk rules." Our ability to talk about feelings is usually affected by the family *rules* we grew up with. Many families live by unspoken rules. Often these include "don't talk rules," especially if alcoholism, other chronic addictions, poverty, or marriage problems were present in our parents' lives. Author Robert Suby describes the consequences of "don't talk" rules in this way:

> *Since we aren't supposed to talk about problems, we begin to believe that if we admit to having problems, then there must be something horribly wrong with us that is not wrong with most people. If we admit to having a problem, we fear we will also be judged by others as weak and unhealthy. Ultimately, this results in a deep sense of shame about a very real part of everyday life, i.e., that we all have problems.*[3]

---

[3] Robert Suby, *Codependency, An Emerging Issue* (Hollywood, FL: Health Communications, Inc., 1984), 26.

Over time and as life unfolds, most families experience difficulties or complications. These elements often give rise to "don't talk" rules within families.

Were there secrets to be kept as you grew up? Did you grow up hearing the phrase, "What will people think?" What were the rules for talking to outsiders about what went on at home? Are the family rules you grew up with making it more difficult for you to share now? Why or why not?

_____
_____
_____
_____
_____
_____
_____
_____
_____

### *Childhood Family Roles*

Another place our new betrayal trauma and the past can intersect pertains to our "roles" in our childhood families. What was your role in your childhood home? Were you the eldest and expected to help hold things together? Were you ignored or devalued in some way? Perhaps you were babied, never having to worry about solving your own problems. (Or maybe you were never allowed.) Sometimes our role in our childhood homes determines our responses to events later in life. What was your role? Do you see any correlation between your childhood role and the way you are now handling your husband's sexual behavior now?

_____
_____
_____
_____
_____

If you are experiencing flashbacks to old traumatic events, or experiencing nightmares, depression, panic attacks, or other complicating factors, find a good counselor who is qualified to help you deal with them. EMDR therapy (Eye Movement Desensitization Reprocessing) is one method that often helps move trauma along the brain's processing pathway more quickly, by engaging both sides of the brain. If the term EMDR is new to you, do an Internet search to learn more. For most people, EMDR proves extremely beneficial, though it may not be available in small towns.

## Losses Related to How We See Ourselves

One of the most important truths you need to embrace is that your partner's behavior is not about you. In fact, regardless of what you may have been told, it has absolutely nothing to do with you. Has anyone tried to blame you, or have you blamed yourself in any way? If so, how? If you have blamed yourself, what can you do to counter that faulty belief system?

_____
_____
_____
_____
_____

For many of us, shifts in self-perception can include now viewing ourselves as naïve, stupid, or rejected. The list of feelings on the Emotional Impact Letter exercise below might help you identify any negative emotions you now harbor about yourself.

Joining Facebook groups for partners of sex addicts can be helpful in reclaiming a healthier view of ourselves, because there you will meet hundreds, perhaps thousands, of other wonderful, often physically beautiful, women who are all going through the same thing. Seeing and interacting with other women makes it easier to realize your husband's betrayal really isn't about you. It's a global epidemic!

## Losses Related to Fear

Early in the healing journey, most of us experience significant levels of fear. Do you have fears because of the betrayal trauma in your life? If so, what do you currently fear?

_____
_____
_____
_____
_____

We don't have to remain powerless in the face of our worst fears. We can turn and face our fears using techniques others have found helpful. We can talk to a safe friend, a support group member, or our therapist, rather than holding our fears in and "keeping them in the dark." By sharing our fears with a safe person whom we trust, we "drag our fears into the light," and expose them to truth. Things always seem more frightening in the dark.

## Consider Journaling

Journaling provides several things we need when we're anxious and stressed. Whether we do it as a daily ritual, or only when we feel overwhelmed, writing down our thoughts and feelings provides a way to "get them out" of our bodies. And because science has shown that thoughts and emotions have an impact at the cellular level, getting them out is an important part of reducing stress and guarding our health.

## Face Our Fears

We can also go straight to the bottom line or worst-case scenario and face the "what if" inside our fears. "What if" the thing we fear actually does happen? What is the worst result we'll experience if it does? By acknowledging the worst possibilities and mapping a plan for how we'll deal with them should they become real, we feel less afraid of the "what ifs." We now have an *insurance plan.* You can read more about approaching our fears in this way in, *You Can Beat Anxiety Without Meds*[4] But if you still experience severe anxiety or panic attacks, and you don't want to take meds, consider buying one of the technological tools HeartMath has created that is helping war veterans beat combat PTSD.

And if you ultimately need meds, know that many of us have needed to ask our doctors for prescription help with these symptoms. PTSD often generates extreme anxiety, and some think the tradeoff is worth the better quality of life that their meds produce.

Dealing with our feelings in a positive way means coming to understand them and where they originate. It means finding healthy ways to cope and self-soothe as we allow ourselves to feel them. And it means sharing them with safe people so they lose their power.

## Feelings Assessment Tool

Using the questions below as a tool to analyze our feelings can also be extremely helpful. I suggest you buy a small spiral notebook that will fit in your purse, then use the questions below to help you deal with strong emotions that hit you anytime of the day or night. As you do, be aware that we often mistakenly label our thoughts as feelings. But feelings are always represented by words that describe an emotion, like those on the feelings list that go with the Emotional Impact Letter below. If your feeling begins with words that sound like this: "I feel like he should….," you can be sure you are talking about a thought. A feeling is an emotion, like anger, hurt, fear, etc., and it's coming from inside *you*.

**Feeling:** _____

1. What triggers this feeling for you? Are there certain times, events, people, or thoughts that tend to activate this emotion? If so, what are they?

---

[4] Marsha Means, MA, *You Can Beat Anxiety Without Meds* (A Circle of Joy Press, 2019,2020).

2. Was this emotion and the way it was to be dealt with something you experienced in your childhood family? If it was, how has that affected your ability to deal with it now?

3. What tools can help you cope with this feeling? Remember, you will gain new tools as we work our way through this workbook together.

4. What can you do to self-soothe in the midst of your painful situation? (Remember, it's okay to ask for support, help, and affirmation. Doing so is an important part of our emotional healing.)

You'll find that writing what you are feeling helps clarify what's going on in you, and makes it easier to determine how to care for yourself in the midst of life as it continues around you.

What can you begin to do now to help yourself deal with your fears so your body can begin to calm down and recover from the trauma?

_____
_____
_____
_____
_____
_____

## Emotional Impact Letter Exercise

Most of us who face the pain of this addiction in our marriages experience a roller coaster of emotions that at times overwhelm us. Which of these feelings have you experienced because of your husband's sexual behavior? On the list below, circle those you can relate to, and use the empty lines to add other emotions you feel that aren't listed. Then, using the feelings words you've circled, write a letter to your husband, expressing the emotional impact his betrayal has had on you. If you find this exercise too overwhelming, simply stop and take steps to care for yourself. You can share the letter in a way that works for you. In your support group, with your therapist, or with your couple's therapist, if you and your husband are still together. Sharing it is an act of courage that helps you find your voice, speak your truth, and take your power back.

*From Betrayal Trauma to Healing & Joy*

| | | | |
|---|---|---|---|
| Abandoned | Weak | Helpless | Lost |
| Isolated | Guilty | Lonely | Conned |
| Hopeless | Depressed | Numb | Invisible |
| Alone | Old | Overwhelmed | Stuck |
| Tired | Confused Sick | Rejected | Used |
| Intimidated | Ashamed | Shocked | Repulsed |
| Afraid | Unattractive | Trapped | Insignificant |
| Stupid | Anxious | Vulnerable | Insulted |
| Empty | Betrayed | Worried | Disgusted |
| Embarrassed | Bitter | Victimized | Naive |
| Inferior | Disappointed | Angry | Disrespected |
| Hurt | Foolish | Sad | Resentful |
| | | Humiliated | Crazy |

_____    _____    _____    _____

_____    _____    _____    _____

## Emotional Impact Letter

_____
_____
_____
_____
_____
_____
_____
_____
_____
_____
_____
_____
_____
_____
_____
_____
_____
_____
_____
_____
_____
_____
_____
_____

**Tasks, Tools & Truths Discussed in this Chapter**

1. Grieving containers
2. The HeartMath exercise
3. Identifying and sorting our emotions for processing
4. Marriage in the digital age
5. Losses due to triggers
6. Losses that hook the past
7. Abandonment
8. Don't talk rules from childhood
9. Childhood family role
10. Losses in how we see ourselves
11. Losses related to fear
12. Feelings assessment tool
13. Writing an Emotional Impact Letter exercise

## APPLICATION: APPLYING TRUTH TO LIFE

From my work in this chapter I realize I need to take the following action steps:

_____
_____
_____
_____
_____
_____
_____
_____
_____
_____
_____
_____
_____
_____
_____
_____
_____

**Graffiti on support group walls...**

I'm so numb I can't fill in the blanks.

*One of the best things I can do is be in touch with my feelings in positive ways.*

# 3

# Personal Empowerment & the Art of Detachment

*This chapter requires two weeks*

## Helpful Supplemental Material

- Read pages 129–131 of *Your Sexually Addicted Spouse*
- Read pages 147–151 of *Your Sexually Addicted Spouse*

When your husband is involved in inappropriate sexual behavior, much of your life is out of your control. You can't count on him to care more about you than his sexual activities, and because your lives are so intimately entwined, his addiction creates chaos in your life too. Even though he may give you his word that he won't act out again, you've likely endured many broken promises. Never knowing when you'll be hurt again is like living through an unending earthquake. The ground beneath your life and marriage constantly shakes and shifts, and nothing remains stable.

Living this way increases your stress, robs your peace, and impacts you at every level of your being. Just as living through an earthquake traumatizes those who endure it, so too does living through this life-quake traumatize its victims. And when we're trauma victims, most of us feel disempowered. We feel helpless and powerless to help ourselves. And when we're disempowered emotionally, we lose our ability to re-stabilize our lives, regain balance, and reclaim peace.

But learning to detach from the emotional turmoil generated by our husbands and their addiction can restore sanity to our lives. Detachment can empower us to face reality and make decisions about our future. Stepping into our *strengths as women* helps us reconnect with ourselves and detach. *If we can learn to do this, we move from a reactive position to a proactive one.*

## Reestablish Your Sense of Power & Control in Your Life

What does it mean to feel disempowered? It means we feel as if we've lost our competence: our adult strength—our power—to manage and direct our own lives.

Because sexual betrayal creates betrayal trauma in those who experience it, it leaves us stranded in the feelings part of our brain. Stranded there, we can feel like a helpless child, powerless to carry on our normal adult lives, even though we may typically be self-confident, self-directed, and ready to tackle the world. Trauma can leave us feeling powerless to move forward, unable to access our normal strengths. Our *capacity* simply isn't great enough to pull us out of the downward spiral set off by betrayal trauma.

Trauma specialists tell us that, along with reestablishing safety, reestablishing our sense of empowerment is essential to heal from trauma. We need to know we have the *power* (the ability) to take care of ourselves and protect ourselves from repeats of the traumatic events. This includes the knowledge we can survive financially, which can prove challenging when we're married and may have let our own career go, because we made commitments to the home and children, thinking that as a team with our partner, we had financial safety.

How *empowered* do you feel right now to manage your life and protect yourself from repeated sexual betrayal? Since discovering your husband's betrayal, have you experienced a sense of powerlessness? If so, where are you currently in relation to that feeling? If 100% = great empowerment and 1% = no empowerment, what percentage represents where you are today?

_____

_____

_____

As betrayed women, several skills play important roles in regaining our sense of empowerment. Developing and strengthening these "tools" augments our capacity and increases our ability to detach from the addict. And as they do, we grow in our ability to navigate the uncharted waters that come with loving a sexual addict.

### *Ingredients of Empowerment for Partners of Sexual Addicts*

1. Self-awareness so we know what we're feeling and what we need.
2. A life-giving, joy-producing support system of safe women
3. The ability to detach when needed.
4. The ability to access our impersonal energy in hyper-emotional situations.
5. The ability to regulate our emotions.
6. Solid grounding to avoid dissociation.
7. Skills to self-soothe and provide good self-care.
8. Healthy boundaries.
9. Healthy conflict-management skills.
10. A financial plan (so you don't have to be a *victim*, should you face repeated betrayals and/or abuse).

We talked about self-awareness in chapter one, and we'll touch on it again later in this workbook. And we'll talk about the others on this list, with the exception of conflict-management skills. If you need help with conflict-management skills—and most of us do—I highly recommend a little book titled, *Speaking Your Mind Without Stepping on Toes*.[5] It's been invaluable to me.

In this chapter we will come to understand and grow in our ability to regulate our emotions, access impersonal energy, ground ourselves (if we begin to dissociate), and detach in order to achieve enough emotional distance to stay calm and secure.

In chapter four, we'll learn how to self-sooth and provide self-care, and talk more about how joy-producing relationships can augment our capacity. In chapter five, we'll learn how to create and use healthy boundaries. Then If you decide you need help with the last two skills on the list, consider joining a group that focuses on gaining healthy conflict management skills and one to help you build a solid financial plan, or work with a specialist in gaining financial independence. Your financial freedom and the ability to reinforce consequences, should the need arise, depend on creating a working financial plan for the future, should your husband continue to make the wrong choices.

## Gaining the Ability to Regulate Our Emotions

Trauma often traps us in unhealthy circular thought patterns, panic responses, and unexpected triggers, leaving us feeling helpless. The limbic system in our brain is on high-alert, and keeps the sympathetic nervous system and the "fight, flight, or freeze response" turned on. As our traumatized brains keep sending out alarm signals—and dumping alarm chemicals—due to the traumatizing experience, our thoughts can spin, and we can act *and react* in ways very unlike ourselves. Many of us get stuck there because we don't know how to regulate erratic, trauma-induced thoughts or emotions when something or someone catches us off guard.

However, our Creator gifted us with a way to bring balance, *if we can access it before we spin out of control*. He created our brains with a prefrontal cortex, and by learning to access it *before* we're spinning, we can regain the strength (capacity) to reason, make deliberate decisions, and recognize the meaning beneath our emotions. And as we learn and grow, we regain some power over our thought patterns.

Some trauma specialists call this switch from the emotion-producing limbic system to the logical, pre-frontal cortex **"down-regulating"** our emotions. Others call it **"emotional agility,"** sort of like emotional gymnastics. Whatever we call it, learning to switch from heightened emotions to calm reasoning is a powerful skill. Thanks to technology, several new apps and tools have been developed, that can help us grow in our ability to "calm" ourselves before it's too late.

Earlier I mentioned the **HeartMath appreciation tool** and its powerful benefits. The scientists at HeartMath have given us a simple appreciation exercise that enables us

---

[5]

synchronize our brain rhythm and heart rhythm to bring what they call "coherence" to our body. And when we use it, a peaceful sense of calm settles our system within two or three minutes. And this exercise can be done anytime, anywhere, and it's absolutely free. And according to their website, if we use it faithfully, we gain an increasing ability to self-regulate.

Another exercise that helps us calm our limbic system is called the **Butterfly Hug.** In *You Can Beat Anxiety Without Meds* I tell you where to go online to learn more about this simple tool that so many find calming, as well as more information about HeartMath and other resources. But try the Butterfly Hug right now by bending your elbows and crossing your forearms over your chest, resting the fingers of your left hand just below the collar bone on the right side of your body, and visa-versa. Then gently tap your fingers. By gently tapping your fingers, you are doing an EMDR[6] exercise that helps calm your body.

Another way to turn down our emotions when our thoughts spin is **to move from our heads to our bodies**, and using some form of movement to balance our system. Here's how one support group member scored a victory by using this tool:

> *Last night I had another terrible nightmare that woke me up crying after connecting with my husband physically. It happens every time we are intimate physically. I woke up at 6:00 a.m. on Saturday morning sobbing and told him about it. Then I put on my running shoes and went for a six-mile hike. I prayed the whole time that God would remove the images from my mind. I came home feeling a ton better and proud of myself, because taking physical action kept the dream from sending me into a tailspin.*

If we intentionally move from our brains to our bodies, we gain some ability to stop *spinning* thoughts and feelings. A body-based activity is any physical activity you enjoy—walking, dancing, listening to uplifting music, biking or something else that gets you out of your head and into your body. It's an intentional choice to *regulate* or rebalance our system. It's like jamming a water wheel with a piece of wood, stopping it mid-cycle. It gives our entire being a break. It's utilizing the benefits of brain/body balance to move toward rebalancing your entire being. Learning to manage emotional pain is an empowering way to live, and it helps us participate in our healing.

Describe a time when you've gotten caught in circular thinking. What did it feel like? Was it easy or difficult to stop your circular thinking? What, if anything, worked for you?

___

[6] Eye Movement Desensitization Reprocessing Therapy

What kind of physical activity could you try for down-regulating next time you get caught in circular thinking? How can you prepare for those spin-cycle times when you need to get out of your head and into your body?

___

## Accessing Our Impersonal Energy

Though the term "impersonal energy" sounds like psychobabble, all of us operate out of both personal and impersonal energy at times. Trauma specialist Tana Slay describes impersonal energy this way:

> *Impersonal energy means to come from an aspect of one's personality which is not bound to one's emotions and feelings. The client is able to step outside his emotions and feelings and view himself and his experience from another perspective. This allows the client freedom in choosing his response to an experience instead of being driven by his unresolved trauma pain and cognitive distortions.*

But the easiest way to understand this form of energy and to locate it inside of you, is to reflect on times in your life when you've had to respond from a rational place in the midst of a crisis to help someone you cared about. Perhaps by sharing such a time from my own life, I can help you recollect a time in your own. My most vivid memory took place when I was a young mother.

I had gone to the mall with a friend, along with my two young children and my friend's son. This mall had low raised platforms where shoppers could sit. For children, they were platforms to jump off of. And that evening, as my friend and I chatted, our children were among the kids jumping off one of those platforms. Then suddenly, my five-year-old son lost his balance and fell face-first against the hard edge of concrete covered with ceramic tile, banging the bone below his eye. Not only did the impact bring tears, it split that part of his face open and blood began to run down his face.

My usual *modus operandi* would be to react in a way charged with emotion—with *personal energy*—rather than with the rational response of *impersonal energy*. But that night, before there were cell phones, my impersonal energy kicked into high gear (I guess because I am a mother). I scooped up my son and shouted to my friend to grab my three-year-old's hand and follow me. We raced through the mall and to the car, and were soon at the hospital.

Though the story eventually ended with only a scar, it nearly cost my son an eye—and his life--when he got a staph infection at the hospital. But thanks to impersonal energy, combined with my faith, I was able to move through the very difficult week that followed from a calm place very unlike myself. This God-given ability to operate out of "impersonal energy"—energy not propelled by my more-typical emotional state—enabled me to arrange child care for my daughter so I could stay at the hospital, call my children's father to come home early from a business trip, notify relatives, call my son's school and kindergarten teacher, and make crucial decisions with the help of his doctors.

I share my experience in the hope it will help you recall a time when you, too, operated out of the calm strength of impersonal energy—to remember how it feels, and more importantly, to help you connect with the space inside you where this kind of energy resides, so you can intentionally access it when needed. For me, moving between personal and impersonal energy works best if I think of it as switching emotional gears. If we can learn to shift from the panic-driven part of ourselves to the calm parts—to our impersonal energy—we have one more tool to use to reclaim our sense of personal empowerment and regain a portion of our emotional strength.

Share a time when you operated out of impersonal energy. Did it enable you to get through a difficult experience that would have been harder if you had a more emotional response? Looking back, how did it feel, either while the experience was happening, or when it was behind you?

_____
_____
_____
_____
_____
_____
_____
_____
_____

Do you think you can find that place inside and *switch to that gear* if, or when, your emotions about your partner's addiction begin to swamp you? How might it help you?

_____
_____
_____
_____

## Dissociation's Role in Disempowerment

For some of us, dissociation also impedes both our ability to gain empowerment over our lives and progress in our healing. And because trauma can cause dissociation, it's important to recognize it, learn how to intercept it, and take action to stay grounded. Doing this important work will speed healing if you struggle with dissociation, though not everyone does.

How can you know if you dissociate? In its mildest form, dissociation feels like your brain has vacated the premises—as if your mind got lost somewhere and only your body is piloting your life. For those who were abused as children, especially sexually, dissociation can be severe and requires a counselor's help to make progress in healing and overcoming dissociation's pull. But even without early trauma, we may at times get lost in a mild form of dissociation when our minds wander off and ruminate about our husband's betrayal. Without meaning to, we totally surrender our thoughts to reliving the pain. That's mild dissociation. Usually we don't even realize it's happening until we find ourselves in that state. Therapists call this "losing grounding," and "losing time."

To process trauma—either recent or historical—and heal from it, we need to employ tools that enable us to process what hurt us, while remaining safe. Grounding provides one safety-keeping tool. If you struggle with dissociation and you're working with a counselor, ask her to teach you how to ground yourself.

## Learning to Ground Ourselves

Solid grounding is the opposite of dissociation. To be grounded is to be present in the moment; mindful of what we're doing and aware of how we're doing on multiple levels. It's the opposite of mentally "checking out," like we do when we drive to some destination and suddenly realize we've traveled miles with no memory of the trip.

Learning to stay present—to be mindful and remain grounded—provides another important tool for growing your empowerment and ability to heal. Grounding ourselves requires that we get in touch with the concrete world around us by feeling the floor beneath our feet, listening to ambient sounds in our environment, looking at the world around us, and generally helping ourselves get back "into" our physical bodies. For more on dissociation, you can read pages 147–151 of *Your Sexually Addicted Spouse*[7]

---

[7] Barb Steffens, PhD, Marsha Means, MA, *Your Sexually Addicted Spouse: How Partners Can Cope and Heal* (Far Hills, NJ: New Horizons Press, 2009.) 147-151.

Do your recall times in your life when you've dissociated? Have you struggled with dissociation since finding out about your husband's betrayal? If so, please share your plan to intercept dissociation so you can engage with a plan for empowerment. If you need help from your group or your counselor, please let them know, because healing requires support.

_____
_____
_____
_____
_____
_____
_____
_____

Many women have never experienced dissociation, but for those of us who have, identifying it, learning to intercept it, then taking action to reground ourselves (as described in *Your Sexually Addicted Spouse*) greatly increases personal empowerment and our ability to heal.

## Gaining the Ability to Detach

Many of us believe that if we try hard enough or pray fervently enough, we can keep our husbands from their addictions. But eventually most of us learn an important, though dreadfully painful, truth: We are powerless to control another person, *especially an addict.* Though we hate it, we must face the fact that we didn't cause this problem, we can't control this problem, and we certainly can't cure it.

When you allow yourself to consider this truth—that you are powerless to prevent your spouse from acting out again—what do you feel? Be honest with yourself.

_____
_____
_____
_____
_____
_____
_____
_____
_____

Most of us feel something close to stark terror when we recognize we truly are powerlessness to control our partner's acting out behavior. And without good detachment skills, much of what we think and do is in reaction to what our husband is doing. Detachment is a skill that helps us step out of that *reactionary* cycle with our husband.

But because our view of ourselves is so tied up in his inappropriate sexual activities, it's very difficult not to react to what he has done (or is doing) sexually. We may shut down emotionally, attack, become verbally abusive, or react in other unhealthy ways. Yet none of these actions will help. They only create ugly scenes and demean us in our partner's eyes. (I know from personal experience.) Yet accepting our powerlessness to control his behavior is not the same thing as accepting whatever he does.

Has it been difficult for you to not take your husband's addiction as being about you?
If so, has it cut into your sense of personal empowerment and your ability to detach? How has that felt for you?

_____
_____
_____
_____
_____

## What is Detachment?*

*I recommend you listen to a free recorded call in which I interview other women on the topic of detachment. You can listen for free by going to my website, clicking on the link, Helpful Resources → Essential Tools → Recorded Calls → Detachment. It can be extremely helpful to learn from women who've walked this path before you.*

As I talk to women about detachment, I often compare this journey to a railroad. I hope train tracks can help you better understand the power of healthy detachment.

Envision yourself standing on a train track in flat, hill-less country. If you look down the tracks just a few feet ahead, the tracks are separate, but held together by railroad ties. But if you look way ahead to the horizon, you will see the tracks appear to merge and become one. This mental image forms a picture of the importance of learning to detach, especially in early recovery.

Early in our recovery, we need to walk our own recovery rail, as does our partner. Without those separate rails, our trauma and the anger it often generates can set off painful conflicts that slow recovery and healing. And should he slip while working his program, it rocks our world. Walking your own rail is important even if he's not yet in recovery, because he will feel the difference and be concerned if you are not hyper-focused on his addiction and behavior. Although at first walking different rails can feel lonely, like the train tracks far on the horizon, the goal is to once again come back together, but with peace. Hold this image as you finish reading.

I recently learned an interesting fact about how train tracks were originally laid, and what I learned helps us better understand how railroad lessons can help us save marriages, if both parties are willing to do the required work.[8]

As workers put the rails and ties in place, a train cart followed behind them. In that train cart were more rails, ties, and the other necessary pieces required to lay train tracks. Because of the cart following behind, the workers had a supply of materials to lay more track in front of them. But here's the best part of the history lesson: workers could not lay new track *unless both rails, the one on the right and the one on the left, were laid down in tandem.* Without that symmetry building the railroad lines would have stopped, because the cart wouldn't have two tracks to move forward on.

And so it is in healing a relationship following betrayal. Even the "victim" needs a way to heal and grow, if she hopes to stay in the relationship. Each partner needs to lay and walk a rail of recovery, and as they do, they move forward in the same direction together.

Learning to detach is much like learning to walk your own rail. Detachment means intentionally putting a space between you and your partner so each of you, for a time, can concentrate on your own individual recovery. Yes, things feel different when you detach, but just like a set of train tracks, you're still close enough to touch. And you're still headed in the same direction. And the ties hold you together, whether the ties in your marriage are committed love, children, dreams you both share—or all three. But you're allowing space—and time—for change, growth, and healing.

If we go further and think of your marriage as the train itself, the importance of staying on your own rail becomes crystal clear. We know from watching the news that if a train doesn't run on two rails, it jumps the tracks and destruction follows. And so does a relationship trying to heal from betrayal trauma require two rails. Repeatedly we've seen that if each partner can't focus on their own recovery rails, especially early in their healing journeys, their relationship derails. At best, healing takes longer; and at worst, the relationship ends in destruction.

But if you can walk your rail, and he can walk his, rest assured that in the future your two rails will converge. Then, with help, you can focus on rebuilding your coupleship. A bit of space now is a small price to pay for a rich and satisfying lifelong relationship.

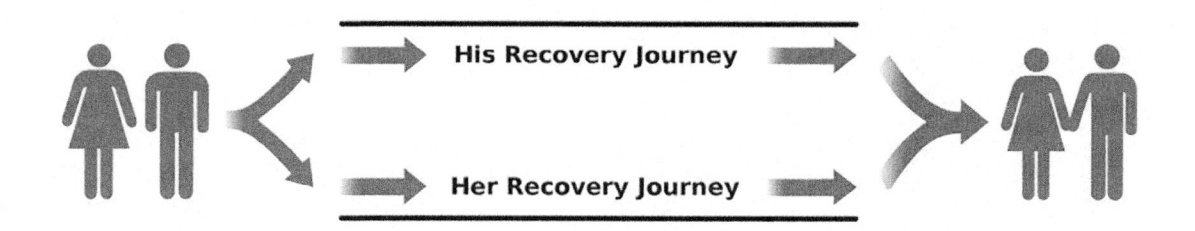

Detaching is not withdrawing. It is not isolating; nor is it punishing. Rather, it is putting a *buffer space* between you and your partner. For me, detaching is like installing a storm

---

[8] I haven't been able to corroborate with research, but I assume this is accurate information.

window over a single pane of glass. A barrier is created between the two panes. I picture that barrier space as being filled with God. I am on one side of the double glass window, and my partner is on the other. God is between us. If every time I begin to react, I think of having to break through that glass and push God out of my way to get to my husband, it helps create a mental barrier for me. It creates a spiritual and emotional buffer between me and the one I love— and between me and any unhealthy reactions.

Detaching is not negative or reactive; it is a positive, proactive step. It enables you to gain objectivity, face reality, deal with your emotions, and determine the best course of action for your life. It doesn't require that you hate your husband or abandon him emotionally. Nor is it something you do once and never need to do again. You'll find that you need to detach again and again and again and again; because when you're triggered, the pain and fear can instantly surface and swamp you. Every time you feel yourself getting hooked or beginning to react, think of having to break that glass and push God out of the way to reach your husband. Whisper a prayer. Leave the room. Call your support or accountability person. Do whatever it takes to stop your racing feelings and thoughts, then calm yourself again.

If the storm window imagery doesn't work for you, use the following space to create your own visual image to use when you get triggered. Just as championship athletes do workouts in their minds to hone their skills, we, too, can mentally practice our preferred responses to situations that will trigger us in the future.

_____
_____
_____
_____
_____
_____
_____
_____

Author Pia Melody, describes healthy detachment as "putting up a wall of pleasantness." What behaviors can you use to create a wall of pleasantness in your relationship with your husband, even if there is emotional or physical distance between you at this time?

_____
_____
_____
_____
_____

*From Betrayal Trauma to Healing & Joy*

When one young wife whose addict husband was not yet in recovery grasped the concept of detachment and found the centeredness and calm it brings, she shared the following vivid description. This is how it felt to her. Perhaps it will help you:

### Detachment

*I see my husband being sucked into a deep, dark pit, desperately grasping at the side with one hand. I cling to his other hand as I frantically try to pull him out. He defiantly believes he can pull himself out, and struggles to free his hand from my grasp. As he struggles, he is pulling me down with him. Detaching is realizing I can do him no good by falling into the pit with him, so I let go, even though I believe he will go deeper. Now, however, I am free to run for help.*

*—Anonymous*

Does it seem wrong or frightening to let go of your husband's hand and give up trying to rescue him? If so, can you explain to yourself why?

_____
_____
_____
_____
_____

The following poem describes the process of letting go—another way to describe detachment:

### Letting Go

*To let go does not mean to stop caring; it means I can't do it for someone else.*

*To let go is not to cut myself off; it's the realization that I can't control another.*

*To let go is not to enable, but to allow learning from natural consequences.*

*To let go is to admit powerlessness—which means the outcome is out of my hands.*

*To let go is not to try to change or blame another; it's to make the most of myself.*

*To let go is not to care for, but to care about.*

*To let go is not to judge, but to allow another to be a human being.*

*To let go is to not be in the middle, arranging all the outcomes, but to allow others to affect their own destinies*

*To let go is not to be protective; it's to permit another to face reality.*

*To let go is not to deny, but to accept.*

*To let go is not to nag, scold or argue, but instead to search out my own shortcomings and correct them.*

*To let go is not to adjust everything to my desires, but to take each day as it comes, and cherish myself in it.*

*To let go is not to criticize and regulate anybody, but to try to become what I dream I can be.*

*To let go is to not regret the past, but to grow and live for the future.*

*To let go is to fear less and love more.*

—*Author Unknown*

What is your reaction to this poem?

_____
_____
_____
_____
_____

Can you *let go* and remain empowered? How does it feel to let go—to acknowledge your powerlessness—while remaining empowered *over your own self?* Remember, detachment is *not* trying to control another. It's taking a step back from making *him* your focus so you can do what you must to enable *yourself* to heal.

_____
_____
_____
_____
_____

As you reflect on the poem and where your husband is right now, what action does it indicate that you should take?

_____
_____
_____
_____
_____
_____
_____
_____

*From Betrayal Trauma to Healing & Joy*

Coming to recognize our powerlessness to control our husband's thoughts and behavior is the first step in letting go of our efforts to control him. And only when we let go can we refocus our attention on helping ourselves become healthier, stronger, empowered women so we can deal with the reality of our situation and begin to heal. But letting go sometimes leaves us feeling vulnerable. *In Women Who Love Too Much*, Robin Norwood captures this distressing feeling:

> *In taking these steps, you will be required to do something from time to time that is very difficult. You will have to face the terrible emptiness within that surfaces when you are not focused on someone else. Sometimes the emptiness will be so deep, you will almost be able to feel the wind blowing through the place where your heart should be. Allow yourself to feel it, in all its intensity, otherwise you'll look for another unhealthy way to distract yourself. Embrace the emptiness and know that you will not always feel this way.*[9]

How do you feel when you read this and reflect on the risk love requires? Is love worth such a high price to you? Why or why not?

_____

_____

_____

_____

_____

_____

_____

_____

Famed author, C.S. Lewis contemplated the above question after the death of his beloved wife. His words poignantly describe the vulnerability loves requires. Is it worth the risk?

*"To love at all is to be vulnerable. Love anything and your heart will be wrung and possibly broken. If you want to make sure of keeping it intact you must give it to no one, not even an animal. Wrap it carefully round with hobbies and little luxuries; avoid all entanglements. Lock it up safe in the casket or coffin of your selfishness. But in that casket, safe, dark, motionless, airless, it will change. It will not be broken; it will become unbreakable, impenetrable, irredeemable. To love is to be vulnerable."*[10]

Detaching from your partner will leave a big hole in your life. Using good self-care and learning to self-soothe, along with nurturing, supportive relationships with other women, provide two of the richest sources of connection and encouragement. In the next chapter we will turn our attention to the roles these tools play in our healing and the ways they boost our personal empowerment.

---

[9] Robin Norwood, *Women Who Love Too Much* (New York, NY: Pocket Books, 1986), 254.
[10] C.S. Lewis, <u>The Four Loves</u>

Detachment requires a quiet, centered strength. It requires recognizing and believing God truly loves you and will never leave you, no matter what circumstances are at work in your life. Can you fully embrace this reality, and detach from your husband and his addiction, clinging to God's hand as you do, believing He will never let go?

As you consider this action step, describe what you feel.

_____
_____
_____
_____
_____
_____
_____
_____

Remind yourself often to practice this important relational skill called detachment.

As you seek to maintain whatever level of detachment your husband's addiction now requires, you may find the Serenity Prayer helpful. It's a wonderful tool to use again and again—to help us embrace our own empowerment while acknowledging our powerlessness over the addict, and entrusting God with the outcome. Use it as often as you need; many have found it a crucial part of their healing and recovery. A framed copy hangs in my office.

> *God, grant me the serenity to accept the things I cannot change, the courage to change the things I can, and the wisdom to know the difference.*
> *—Reinhold Niebuhr*

## Tasks, Tools & Truths Discussed in this Chapter

1. Learning how to reestablish our power and control over our own lives
2. Ingredients of empowerment
3. Gaining the ability to regulate our emotions
4. Accessing our impersonal energy
5. Understanding dissociation's role in disempowerment
6. Grounding ourselves
7. Gaining the ability to detach
8. Letting go

# APPLICATION: APPLYING TRUTH TO LIFE

From my work in this chapter, I realize I need to take the following action steps:

_____
_____
_____
_____
_____
_____
_____
_____
_____
_____
_____
_____

## Graffiti from Support Group Walls

I'm so numb I can't fill in the blanks.

*How do I become a separate person? In my family growing up, I wasn't allowed to have my own feelings. Calling it my "codependency" feels sticky; it makes me part of the pain. Traumatized honors the pain and who I am in it.*

**I'm not his parent; I love him, but I won't do it for him.**

Fear, anger, silence, and strong words are walls; we need to use boundaries that are not walls. I can always respond to my partner the way I do to my neighbors when I see them: I'm pleasantly appropriate.

*I refuse to react in anger or revenge. These are walls. But a veil of pleasantness does not mean that I have to suffer. I need to use my veil out of love for myself when I need it. If I am in the house and making dinner, I make his as well. If he wants to kiss me, I give him my cheek.*

For me, it's stepping back and observing.
**I find detachment can be as slippery as mercury from a broken thermometer.**

*Love should not require us to let go parts of ourselves.*

**I can think of my wall of pleasantness as respect for him as a fellow human being, and it will help me detach.**

*It means I need to stay warm and on my side of the line.*

It means becoming my own hero.   I can let go and not "go away"

*From Betrayal Trauma to Healing & Joy*

# 4

# Self-Care & Self-Soothing for Empowerment: Part I

*This chapter requires two weeks*

## Helpful Supplemental Material if You Have Time

- Read Chapters 7 and 8 of *Your Sexually Addicted Spouse*.

## The Importance of Secure Attachment in Our Healing

Children who grow up in ideal situations realize they are not alone in the world, because they consistently—at least most of the time—receive comfort and soothing from loving adults who are an important part of their lives. Generally, childhood equips them to find healthy, safe people to support them through painful events and difficult times. These abilities carry over into adulthood, and enable them to understand, tolerate, and manage their overwhelming feelings, or to get help when they can't. And they usually recognize the untruths or false beliefs they encounter; false beliefs like, "I must not be enough for him or he wouldn't have betrayed me." Drawing on Attachment Theory, we say their *attachment needs* were met by their primary caregivers.

Children in these situations bring a secure sense of their worth and value into adulthood. They feel good about who God created them to be. And if they someday experience betrayal trauma in their primary relationship, they know it's not about them. This security equips them with sufficient emotional capacity, which we talked about in Chapter One.

However, few of us grow up in ideal situations. When our capacity is low due to a difficult childhood, or life-shattering events as an adult, we may have difficulty coping with life's stresses. We're not good at self-care and self-soothing, and we don't usually proactively find the help we need. These skills, along with self-esteem and others, tend to be impaired. When disaster strikes, we feel completely overwhelmed and can't determine what to do.

For people who missed out on a healthy childhood, gaining the skills needed to heal from betrayal trauma requires learning new ways of thinking and living, then practicing those ways until they become our own. Throughout this workbook we encourage a mind-set that leads to viewing yourself as a victor, rather than a victim. As one who not only survives, but thrives. But that requires healing and eventual transformation, if secure attachment was missing in your childhood.

As you look back on your growing up years, how did they impact your emotional capacity? Did you experience painful traumas, such as a parent's death, or physical, emotional, or sexual abuse? Even the absence of adequate love can create trauma in a child. Or were you blessed growing up, secure in your parents' love and mostly free of tragedy?

_____
_____
_____
_____
_____
_____
_____
_____

From where you are in life right now, how do you rate your ability to do good selfcare and self-soothe for comfort? What is your emotional capacity? If 100% represents doing these things extremely well, and 1% represents not doing them at all, what percentage represents your ability to self-soothe and do self-care at this time in your life? And to what do you attribute your current percentage?

_____
_____
_____
_____
_____
_____
_____

## Capacity

Have you ever seen an electrical outlet with a multi-plug adapter trying to provide power for five or six different small appliances? It looks like a fire waiting to happen, doesn't it?

Many of us feel like that overloaded outlet, so overwhelmed we're ready to throw a breaker; or worse, catch fire. Even when we typically have plenty of capacity, this particular heartbreak can push us beyond what we can bear and totally max us out. It can leave us feeling disempowered, and we find it hard to cope, much less do good self-care.

Stop and think about that overloaded outlet for a moment. If this mental image describes the way you feel much of the time, *how many appliances* are currently plugged into you?

How close are you to throwing a breaker, or worse, catching fire? How does it feel to be *you* right now?

_____
_____
_____
_____
_____
_____
_____
_____

Regaining our empowerment—our sense of control over our safety and lives—requires *increasing our capacity*. In this chapter, we talk about a variety of ways to increase your capacity so it becomes possible for you to heal.

## Increasing Your Capacity Through Life-Giving Relationships

One of the best ways to increase our capacity is to increase our "joy strength." And this kind of joy-strength comes from supportive relationships. The Life Model clinicians tell us just how important our joy strength is to our healing:

> *If a person in recovery is not empowered by joy, it may be impossible to face the pain that is part of recovery. In fact, the amount of joy strength available needs to be higher than the amount of pain. Therefore, building joy through life-giving relationships is often the first part of recovery.*[11]

After decades of treating victims of traumatic experiences, Shepherd's House Counseling Center in Pasadena, California, began studying why some clients healed and others didn't. Their findings revealed that those with loving, supportive, joy-producing relationships *outside of therapy* consistently healed; and those without joy-based relationships didn't. From their work, they developed the Life Model, now taught to clinicians and addiction specialists around the world.

But there's more. Listen to this:

> *We now know that a "joy center" exists in the right orbital prefrontal cortex of the brain (right behind your right eye). It has executive control over the entire emotional system. When the joy center has been sufficiently developed, it regulates emotions, pain control, and immunity centers; it guides us to act like ourselves; it releases neurotransmitters like dopamine and serotonin. . . .*[12]

---

[11] Shepherd's House, *The Life Model* (Pasadena, CA: lifemodel.org, 2009), 23.
[12] Shepherd's House, Inc., *The Life Model* (Pasadena, CA: lifemodel.org, 2009), 23.

**And we can actually make it grow—even if we are adults! The study of living brains shows both traumatized and addicted brains can literally rewire the connections in the joy center of the brain** *as people participate in joy-bonded relationships.*

Wow! Imagine that. You have a place in your brain—just behind your right eye— that you can utilize to help you make it through this horrific pain. Isn't that amazing? Let's talk about some practical ways to put this brain science to work so you can heal and go on to thrive for the remainder of your life.

But to fully utilize joy-power, we need to understand how Attachment Theory and joy-producing relationships intersect.

*(If you would like to learn more about attachment theory and how it can transform lives and marriages, read the books in the footnote at the bottom of this page.*[13]*)*

## Attachment Bonds & Capacity Formed in Infancy

When a mother looks at her baby with adoration, her eyes reflect to the baby that she delights *in him, and he has value. As she does, her baby feels joy, and positive self-esteem and emotional capacity begin to form in him.* This is how attachment theory and joy intersect. *Humans feel joy when they are adored or cherished.* But even if you missed that kind of childhood, it's never too late to mend attachment wounds or deficits through new, life-giving, joy-producing relationships. It requires intentionality, but it can be done.

## Joy in Adulthood Requires Intentionality

Let's push up our sleeves and talk about how you can increase your joy-strength and capacity by utilizing or building joy-filled relationships.

## Intimate Joy-Filled Relationships

How many joy-producing relationships do you have in your life right now? Only count relationships that are real—relationships that go below the surface of life, relationships with people who know your heartaches and struggles, yet still love and accept you for who you truly are. If you come up short, what <u>intentional</u> things can you do now to begin working on growing deep, safe relationships with one or two women?

_____

_____

_____

_____

---

[13] Joy Starts Here (Joy Starts Here: the transformation zone, a Life Model Works book) Paperback – 2013 by E. James Wilder ; Tim Clinton, PhD, Gary Sibcy, PhD, Attachments: Why You Love, Feel, and Act the Way You Do (Orange County Integrity Publishing, 2002).

## A Caring, Joy-Filled Community

Do you have a caring, joy-filled community? A group of people with whom you belong? People who know you and miss you if you don't show up? People who will be there to help when you need it? For many of us, our faith-based community provides this joy-foundation, but it might be a different group for you. Perhaps a volunteer position at an organization that stirs your passion, or a club of some sort. If you don't have a caring, joy-filled community in your life already, what intentional steps can you take to find a group where you can belong?

One recent client in particular has done a stellar job of intentionally finding and developing joy-based relationships in a new town, where she is starting over from scratch, all on her own. After decades of marriage and betrayal trauma, and trying to make her marriage work, she knew she had to leave the marriage to save herself. But because of how her husband operates, she also knew she needed distance, while staying in the same state for the sake of her career. The first time I talked to her, my heart ached for the situation she was in, and I felt concerned about what she was going through alone in a new area. But now, just four months later, she provides a phenomenal example of what it takes to create community under difficult circumstances.

Because this woman's faith is an integral part of her life, she began by finding a church that suited her well. And right away, she joined a week-night small group that meets in someone's home. Then she began to develop individual relationships, both with women at work and women in her week-night small group. In addition, she joined a phone group with me, and within a short amount of time, nearly every evening of the week was filled with new friends who provide support and encouragement. She knew that she needed to not be home alone, during the especially difficult first months of beginning life again, but now alone.

Like happens to nearly all of us, she ran into someone who turned out not to be safe, but she didn't let that stop her. She simply moved on. She continued her search for enough safe people to provide "family" in her new town and new life. Then last week, she topped it off by adding a new kitten to keep her company. I have marveled at how far she has come in such a short amount of time. It obviously required a lot of "intentionality," but it worked!

*From Betrayal Trauma to Healing & Joy*

I hope her example will give you ideas and produce new energy to follow her lead. But joy-based relationships can prove difficult to find, at least in western civilizations. That's why finding them requires intentionality. But when your heart is breaking, developing new, joy-based relationships can prove challenging. For that reason, the easiest place to begin could be within your local recovery community. Whether that's a local 12 step group, a Celebrate Recovery group, DivorceCare, or something else, it's easy to find and grow connections in small communities where people want to connect and also want to recover.

Building joy-based relationships into your life is a very important part of your healing journey. If you need to work on this aspect of healing, what steps will you commit to take in the next week to get started?

_____
_____
_____
_____
_____

## Self-Care & Self-Soothing for Empowerment: Part II

As we've progressed through this workbook, we've been learning to use an array of tools that equip us to heal. And that process continues as we move into Part II of this chapter. We're going to tackle some of the biggest challenges we face in our healing, and some of the tools we talk about here are defensive, while others are offensive. A defensive example is one many sex addicts are taught: shouting the word "Stop!" at negative, intrusive thoughts

While shouting "Stop!" at taunting self-talk can help block negative thoughts and help retrain our minds, self-soothing provides a different way to fight trauma. The former is akin to teaching your six-year-old daughter Taekwondo to empower her for life. Whereas the latter is like reading her stories at bedtime, praying with her, then tucking her in and kissing her good night. Each will help her grow up knowing she's loved, competent, and can take care of herself. But if she has both, she'll be much better armed for the tough times she'll face in her journey through life.

So it is when we practice both defensive and offensive measures to help counter trauma's toll on our lives. An important example of an offensive tool is the topic of the next several paragraphs. I encourage you to use it to take care of yourself, even as we talk about some of the greatest challenges we face in our effort to heal, including gaslighting and triggers.

## Use Your Maternal Instinct to Self-Soothe & Comfort Yourself

As women, our Creator gifted us with powerful maternal instincts that we've all used to soothe and comfort others. However, few among us were taught to use these gentle, loving instincts to soothe and comfort ourselves when we are afraid or wounded, sick or tired. Now is the time to turn this valuable gift on ourselves.

Self-soothing creates a buffer between us and the trauma. Remember the storm window image from the last chapter? The space between the two panes of glass creates a buffer; a space. And right now we need a space between ourselves and our fears and grief. Self-soothing activities help provide that buffer. They create a cushion of "time out"—a respite—from the droning drill of the fear and pain. They provide a respite from the toll trauma takes on our spirits, minds, and bodies.

## What Helps You Self-Soothe and Relax?

What helps one may not work for another, but often the things that soothe us are repetitive in nature. Things like rocking in a chair while listening to a book on tape, stroking our cat or petting our dog, needle work of any kind, or playing a musical instrument may help us relax. Other options might include activities that soothe our senses—things like a long bike ride in nature, a walk in nature, cross country skiing in the still of a snow-covered forest, a bubble bath with music and candlelight, a massage, or walking on a beach to the sound of the sea.

What things comfort and soothe you? Are you already doing some of these activities or others you find helpful? Or is self-soothing a new idea you need to try until you find the best method for you? Make a list of activities that work for you and leave space to write down new ideas.

_____
_____
_____
_____
_____
_____
_____
_____
_____

As others in your group share answers to these questions, jot down ideas you haven't yet tried; then, test them to see if they soothe you.

## Gaslighting: Truth Vs. Lies

You have more than likely read the term "gaslighting," but even if you haven't, you've almost certainly experienced it at some time during your experience with betrayal trauma.

Wikipedia defines gaslighting this way:

> *"Gaslighting is a form of psychological manipulation in which a person seeks to sow seeds of doubt in a targeted individual or in members of a targeted group, making them question their own memory, perception, and sanity. Using persistent denial, misdirection, contradiction, and lying, gaslighting involves attempts to destabilize the victim and delegitimize the victim's beliefs."*

Virtually all of us whose husbands have used gaslighting to deflect our attention from their sexually addictive activities failed to recognize it for what it was initially. That means most of us have lived with the crazy-making for months, perhaps years, before reality finally broke through our lack of understanding. But by the time we wake up to reality, a lot of damage can already have been done. Many of us question our judgement, our stability, our intuition—and even our sanity—before the light of truth finally dawns.

One of the most damaging aspects of gaslighting is the way it skews the truth about who we are. Even when we tell ourselves, *"My husband's behavior has nothing to do with me,"* it's extremely challenging not to feel "less than" the 23-year-old babe who works in his office. "When we are wounded, we come to wrong conclusions about ourselves and our world,"[14] says psychiatrist Dr. Karl Lehman. That's one reason we need each other to speak truth into our lives about who we really are.

## Reclaiming & Owning Our True Value

A. Has your husband's betrayal caused you to see yourself differently than you did before? If so, does this changed view show up in the form of negative self-talk? How did you see yourself prior to discovery or disclosure? And how do you see yourself now? List three action steps you can take at least once every day to regain—or build—a healthier view of yourself. If you need help, ask your support group to share ideas with you.

or

B. If your husband's addictive behavior *hasn't* colored your view of yourself, what do you think enabled you to avoid this common trap?

As you consider these questions, remember that our childhood history often gets pulled into how we respond to gaslighting. So if you're struggling to retake ground lost to the crazy-making, work hard to tell yourself your the truth. You are a precious daughter of the King of the Universe; a creation of the Master Designer Himself.

_____
_____
_____
_____

---

[14] Shepherd's House, Inc., *The Life Model* (Pasadena, CA: lifemodel.org, 2009), 86.

_____
_____
_____
_____
_____

## The False Beliefs in Our Negative, Intrusive Thoughts

Like hungry bears displaced by a forest fire, negative, intrusive thoughts sneak into our minds and upset our peace. We're usually not aware of their presence until they've taken over our thoughts and let out a frightening roar. But if we learn techniques to *roar back*, we can reclaim our mental landscape and maintain our peace.

## Shouting "Stop!"

Earlier I said that several authors suggest you shut your eyes and interrupt your intrusive thoughts or images by mentally saying "Stop!" Dr. Milton Magness takes it a step further, suggesting you literally shout the word, "Stop!" out loud while holding your arm out and hand up like a policeman stopping traffic, simultaneously envisioning a stop sign.[15] This practice might even stop a *real* bear.

## Thought Replacement

Another technique is to replace negative thoughts with positive ones. If we envision our future as old and alone, we can just as easily imagine a positive version. A helpful replacement thought might be to imagine yourself walking a beach holding hands with your husband in your sunset years. Or envisioning yourself on a cruise with a few of your closest girlfriends. Science has shown that we move toward that which we envision, so take responsibility for what you see in your future.

## Butterfly Hug and HeartMath Exercise

In Chapter 3 we learned how to use the Butterfly Hug, as well as the HeartMath Appreciation Exercise. If you struggle with negative, intrusive thoughts, have peace-robbing fears, or hear old tapes of gaslighting in your head, I suggest you read, *You Can Beat Anxiety Without Meds,* and try various tools and practices in it. Hopefully at least one of them will enable you to regain peace, and to step into your empowerment. My personal favorite is using the HeartMath tool of appreciation, coupled with breathing "from the heart," as they suggest.

---

[15] Milton S. Magness, DMin, *Thirty Days to Hope and Freedom from Sexual Addiction* (Carefree, AZ: Gentle Path Press, 2010), 112.

Do you struggle with negative, intrusive thoughts? If you do, can you share some here? As you consider the tools you've learned so far, which tools will you test and practice this week, in your effort to win your war for healing and peace?

___

If you've listed untruths you've believed and fears that taunt you, remember to share your list with safe, caring people like those in a support group. Let people who care about you and understand the betrayal reflect truth into your life. Loosening the hold false beliefs have on your heart and mind requires support and team effort.

## Our Fears: Fact or Fiction?

Learning to tell the difference between truth and lies is paramount for your healing journey. For many of us, our false beliefs generate a whole choir of new fears. In jarring discord, they taunt us with "what ifs":

- What if he doesn't want to change? I'll never be able to take care of myself and the kids.
- What if he chooses another woman over me? He's taken my youth, and I'll end up growing old all alone.
- What if he relapses five years down the road? By then I'll be too old to put together an adequate retirement fund to cover my senior years without our joint savings and investments.

Identify and list the "what ifs" in your life.

___

In reality, we know our "what ifs" are powered by our fears and unbridled imaginations. Nonetheless, the truth is that some of our "what ifs" could actually come true. My own story is proof of that. The challenge is to focus on living one day at a time, cloaking ourselves in faith, while simultaneously working hard to prepare for possible unwanted outcomes. What can you do to live one day at a time, while reclaiming your empowerment so you're prepared, no matter what the future brings? We'll talk about the practical parts of this action step in a minute. But for now, what can you do to help your mind and body "calm" so you can care for yourself in the midst of your concerns? Things like practicing yoga, mindfulness, therapy....What will help you?

## A Calming & Empowering Exit Plan

Because so many of our fears are based in our financial security, and our ability to support ourselves and our children if our marriages end, creating a marriage *exit plan* is both empowering and practical. Some of the best-known sexual addiction specialists require partners of sexual addicts to complete this exercise. The intention is not to encourage you to leave your husband. It's to help you relax enough to stay and give your husband an opportunity to prove his desire for true recovery and change—and to help you sleep at night!

If you are not financially self-sufficient (and few mothers are), what action step can you take this week to begin your exit plan? Can you commit to taking some time each week between now and the end of your group to develop your plan for gaining the ability to provide sufficient income, if you should need to?

NOTE: Seeking counsel for guidance about child support laws in your state, province, or country can help you know whether your husband would be required to help financially if your marriage ends. Though you will hopefully never need to use your exit plan, the relief and calm it provides will help you feel empowered, so you can give your husband and marriage a chance to heal.

Most areas now have some kind of Women's Resource Centers, though the name may vary from country to country, so you may need to work to find what you're looking for. Sometimes they are attached to a local college; sometimes to the Better Business Bureau, or another civic organization. If you cannot locate this resource, your doctor may have information to share with you, as can a service like The Crisis Line, which is a 24-hour, free phone support line that is linked to a data base of all kinds of support services. Again, it may have a different name, depending on where you live.

The idea is to find a service that can help you consider your options for financial independence via training programs or possible home-based businesses to support yourself and your children, should the need ever arise.

How do you feel as you consider this exercise?

_____
_____
_____
_____

My Exit Plan (If Needed):

_____
_____
_____
_____
_____
_____
_____
_____
_____
_____
_____
_____
_____
_____
_____
_____

## Taking Happiness Time-Outs

When we're in a lot of emotional pain, we often forget, or even lose interest, in finding moments of happiness and fun. Emotional pain leads us to isolate, to stay in bed when possible, and to avoid the things that used to bring light into our lives.

But just as creating containers for grieving gives us permission to grieve for a certain window of time, happiness time-outs give us much-needed permission to take breaks from our pain. We've learned we can schedule grieving times, but we can also—and should—schedule times to connect with life. These times probably won't produce the delight they previously did because you're still in emotional pain. But even small efforts toward fun and happiness counter isolation and let rays of light and hope into our day and our hearts.

Below is a list of happiness time-out activities generated by other partners over the years. Add ideas or methods of your own, as well as ideas shared by other women in your support group.

- Calling a friend, or going to lunch with a friend
- Breaking isolation by getting out of the house
- Working out, especially to upbeat music
- Listening to music, especially praise or another favorite
- Going for a walk with friends
- Going for a run
- Reading something you enjoy
- Renting a good movie and watching it with friends or loved ones
- Spending time in nature: reading by a lake, hiking, or other outdoor activity
- Going for a bike ride
- Singing with friends or in church
- Dancing
- Playing a musical instrument
- Taking part in your favorite sport
- Playing with children
- Playing fetch with a dog
- Taking a child out for an ice cream cone
- Swinging, climbing a tree, or playing catch with children or a playful friend
- Going to the zoo with a friend or children
- Roller blading, skateboarding, or some other *young-at-heart* sport
- Flying kites with friends or children
- Blowing bubbles

*From Betrayal Trauma to Healing & Joy*

- _____
- _____
- _____
- _____
- _____
- _____

Choose three items from the above list and commit to do them this week to add happiness breaks to your life. Ideally, we should do one activity each day to take a timeout from the pain. Share your three choices with your group.

1. _____
2. _____
3. _____

## Learning Safe, Healthy Ways to Express Strong Feelings

It's also helpful to find healthy ways to express strong, negative feelings. Instead of raging at the one who hurt us, hitting them, or giving them the silent treatment for days, we can choose healthier ways to vent our feelings. This can drain away enough negative emotion to enable us to think through anger and express it in a healthier way.

Each time we make the choice to express and process our feelings in less toxic ways, the hostile, destructive response patterns grow weaker, and our emotions become easier to manage. This frees us to be angry, while expressing our anger in healthier ways, and using it to produce the changes we need.

## Action Steps for Change

However, it isn't easy to be this emotionally healthy. Taking action steps *before we become swamped by strong emotion* is the best way to deal with difficult feelings and circumstances. But that's not easy to do. Find positive methods that work for you by experimenting until you find the best fit. Below is a list of healthy action steps other partners of sexual addicts have found helpful. Add your own in the spaces provided.

- Throw darts at a dart board—vehemently.
- Scribble your feelings until they are spent; you might be surprised by how many pieces of paper you go through in the process.
- Take your rage out on the bed with a pillow or plastic baseball bat.
- Write your partner an *anger letter*, letting yourself yell on paper.
- Sit in your car with the windows rolled up and vent.

- Utilize the power of physical release by running, throwing a ball against an outside surface, or doing some other high-exertion sport like tennis or aerobic dancing.
- Kickbox.
- Use a boxer's punching bag.
- Clean your home
- _____
- _____
- _____
- _____
- _____
- _____
- _____
- _____

The next time life offers you opportunity to try this exercise, turn back to this page and record how it felt and whether or not it helped you productively manage your anger. And if you and your partner currently live together, record his reaction to your proactive venting your strong anger before talking to him.

_____
_____
_____
_____
_____
_____

## Using A God Box

Pictures pack power in the human experience; and a *God Box* provides a concrete container for the fears, hurts, and doubts that overtake us. When we simply don't know what to do with our burdens, when even prayer leaves us feeling their weight, we can write them down and put them in our God Box. Safely tucked inside, our action provides a visual form of prayer, a way to surrender to God those things that especially trouble us.

Some women choose to buy a special container for this purpose; not too large, but something beautiful or particularly meaningful to them. You might choose a small jewelry box, or an especially beautiful small box or tin from an import store. Or, cover a shoe box in beautiful paper or fabric. The box can take on even more meaning if you photocopy meaningful photographs from your life, then use these copies of your photos to cover the box.

A God Box provides a visual representation that God help's us carry our burdens, when we must wait for our prayers to be answered.

## Focus and Faith

Author Louis Tice teaches, "What you hold in your mind is what you move toward." He's dubbed this observation, the *Law of Focused Attention*. Why not put this Law of Focused Attention to work for greater peace now and the hope of a happier future? It is possible to face the unknown realistically, while considering even negative potential outcomes, if we focus our attention on the truth that God is always with us. Never are we truly alone. We can use the Law of Focused Attention to forecast a joy-filled future, whether or not our marriages survive. Isn't that what faith is all about? A much-loved Bible verse tells us that *"Faith is the confidence that what we hope for will actually happen; it gives us assurance about things we cannot see."*[16] Whether we call it faith, or choose to call it imagination, it serves us best by putting it to positive use in our lives.

Each of our lives looks different. What does faith look like for you in your situation?

_____
_____
_____
_____
_____

## Tasks, Tools & Truths Discussed in this Chapter

1. Secure attachment and capacity
2. The power of joy-filled relationships
3. Creating intentional joy
4. Self-soothing and self-comfort
5. Gaslighting: truth vs. lies
6. Finding and reclaiming your "self"
7. False beliefs and negative, intrusive thoughts
8. The "What if's?"
9. Creating an exit plan
10. Happiness time-outs
11. Safely expressing strong feelings
12. A God Box
13. The role faith plays

---

[16] Hebrews 11:1; *The New Living Translation of the Bible*, 2007.

## APPLICATION: APPLYING TRUTH TO LIFE

From my work in this chapter I realize I need to take the following action steps:

_____
_____
_____
_____
_____
_____
_____
_____
_____
_____

## A Spiritual Intervention to Counter Untruths

For those among us who can draw on their faith in God, psychiatrist Karl Lehman says:

*Jesus is the most powerful and most effective source of truth when it comes to correctly interpreting the meaning of an experience, and especially when it comes to replacing distorted, erroneous interpretations with truth.*[17]

Dr. Lehman uses a form of healing prayer, which he calls the Immanuel Approach, in his work with traumatized patients. As he does, people heal and gain the confidence of knowing their traumatic experiences have nothing to do with who they are. Their perspective on past events changes, and the painful memory is *processed* through the necessary regions of the brain, much as EMDR moves or processes painful memories. The end result provides resolution—or what we call integration—of the traumatic event into our larger life story. Now, simply a part of our personal history, the trauma has lost its sting.

If you would like to know more about how you can benefit from this same form of healing prayer, it is available through some of our coaches at **www.ACircleofJoy.com**. Currently two women on our team, Jodi and Katherine, are trained and skilled in helping women utilize this healing modality—even via the phone. You can also learn more at Dr. Lehman at his website, **www.kclehman.com**.

---

[17] Karl Lehman, MD, *Brain Science, Emotional Trauma, and the God Who is With Us* ( www.kclehman.com: 2011)

# 5

# Boundaries

*This chapter requires two weeks*

## Helpful Supplemental Reading if You Have Time:

- *Moving Beyond Betrayal: The 5-Step Boundary Solution for Partners of Sex Addicts,* by Vickie Tidwell-Palmer.

## Boundaries: A Key to Empowerment

Coming to understand boundaries—and learning how to use them wisely and well—is perhaps the single most empowering thing we can do as women, whether or not we are in a relationship with a sex addict. If we divorce, we need this skill. If our relationship survives, boundaries remain essential. Healthy boundaries empower us not only in intimate relationships, but in all relationships. Therapist Vicki Tidwell Palmer says, "Safety is a fundamental human need—and safety is created by the effective use of boundaries."[18]

Yet boundaries are very often misunderstood. Boundaries are not something we do, or try to do, to another person. Nor are they rules about another's behavior, addiction, or recovery program. Rather we craft boundaries to take care of ourselves. Yes, the one you love has wounded you. But trying to control him and calling it a boundary will not only fail to give you the safety you seek; setting boundaries in an effort to control him will also drive him away from you.

## Our Boundaries Usually Develop from Our Life Experiences

The kinds of boundaries we have when we reach adulthood generally depend on how we grew up and experienced life. If boundaries were never allowed in our childhood home, we may be boundary-less. Or once we are grown, we may over compensate and build rigid boundaries in an attempt to protect ourselves from others. Nearly all of us

---

[18] Vicki Tidwell Palmer, LCSW, CSAT, *Moving Beyond Betrayal: The 5-Step Boundary Solution for Partners of Sex Addicts* (Las Vegas, NV: Central Recovery Press, 2016), 31.

have room for improvement when it comes to boundaries, because using boundaries well proves challenging.

We can make our boundaries too rigid and not allow anyone to get close to us. Or we can make them too weak, leaving us vulnerable to abuse. Ideally, our boundaries are permeable, meaning others can reach us if we want them to. When we have permeable boundaries, we choose who to let into our private world, and who to keep out. If people seem safe or trustworthy, we may choose to let them get close to us by sharing our reality with them. If they don't seem safe and trustworthy, we make our boundaries firmer to protect ourselves from hurt or harm.

As you think about your life in general, what kind of boundaries do you think you have? And where do you think your present boundaries originated? Explain below.

_____
_____
_____
_____
_____

## Boundaries: An Important Aspect of Self-Care

Boundaries also provide our greatest form of self-care and personal responsibility. Drs. Cloud and Townsend say it well when they write, "An important aspect of setting boundaries with ourselves is that of taking ownership of our lives. We need to take responsibility for our hearts, our loves, our time, and our talent."[19]

We also need to take responsibility for our healing, and boundaries enable us to do just that.

Boundaries are simply limits. Limits we set *with* ourselves, and limits we set *around* ourselves to maintain safety in our relationships with others. Though we generally think of boundaries in terms of limits we place to protect us from others, boundaries with ourselves are just as important. And this is especially true when we've been wounded by betrayal trauma, because boundaries with ourselves can help us heal.

***Boundaries we set with ourselves can include, among others:***

- Stopping negative self-talk.
- Limiting exposure to triggers so our nervous systems can return to calm.
- Giving ourselves "happiness time-outs" to help balance our lives.
- Countering cognitive distortions.

---

[19] Henry Cloud, PhD, John Townsend, PhD, *Boundaries In Marriage Workbook* (Grand Rapids: Zondervan, 2000), 50.

- Creating temporary time-outs from our pain with meditation or some other calming activity.
- Blocking certain stressors so we can heal.
- Managing our anger so we don't become aggressive with the addict or others.
- Attending support groups to help ourselves heal.
- Learning healthy ways to manage depression or other difficult emotions and getting help, if needed.
- Creating grieving containers, if needed, so we can give ourselves time and space to grieve as life goes on.

Most of the things you learned as you worked through chapters three and four of this workbook involved boundaries with yourself to help you heal. Detaching, letting go, getting grounded to avoid dissociation, gaining the ability to regulate your emotions, taking time to intentionally build joy into your life, learning healthy ways to handle strong emotions—all these and more require you to say no to some things so you can say yes to others.

Boundaries with ourselves require huge effort, especially as we begin making changes in our lives. But if we will take our recovery as seriously as we want our husbands to take theirs, boundaries will enable us to heal. ISA, a 12-step trauma-focused partners' support group based in Houston, Texas, has a self-care checklist on their site that is a useful tool for helping you check and monitor your self-care boundaries. You can find the list at www.isurvivors.org —> Tools —> Self-Care Checklist. As you learn to take responsibility, and care for yourself by using self-boundaries, you will find they are more than worth the hard work they require because they will empower you to care for yourself in all your relationships.

As you look at the bulleted list above, and the checklist at www.isurvivors.org, consider areas in your life where you need to focus more attention to better care for yourself and manage your trauma and emotions. Then list them below.

_____
_____
_____
_____
_____
_____
_____

## Boundaries Role in Dealing with Your Trauma Triggers

For most of us, triggers and triggering situations stand out as the most challenging aspect of recovering from betrayal trauma. However, boundaries can help us plan for, and navigate, known triggers. Or to choose to avoid them altogether. Listing your known triggers and planning for them is an extremely important part of self-care.

Begin taking control of your triggers and trigger-responses by dividing them into two categories:

1. People, places, events, or things you know trigger your trauma.
2. Unexpected, surprise triggers that are difficult to plan for.

Identifying and predetermining how to deal with the first kind of triggers is not only empowering, but also helpful in reducing pain and emotional upheaval so you can make progress and heal. Begin by listing those people, places, events or things you know trigger your trauma. List everything that comes to mind, and in the weeks ahead, add to your list as new thoughts about triggers come to mind.

**Known Triggers**

1. _____
2. _____
3. _____
4. _____
5. _____
6. _____
7. _____
8. _____
9. _____
10. _____
11. _____
12. _____

Now, with healing as your primary goal, think through each of the triggers you've listed above, and determine how you want to deal with it when you encounter it. If historically, you've wrestled with allowing yourself to say "no," even when you really want to, you may struggle with this exercise. Keep in mind that your healing is *your* responsibility. Your answers don't have to be set in stone; you can modify an answer as you see and feel healing happening inside you. But for now, as an important part of self-care, taking measures to reduce trauma-triggering events will enable you to heal with less emotional chaos. So list the ways you plan to manage known triggers.

## How I Will Deal with Known Triggers

1. _____
2. _____

3. _____
4. _____
5. _____
6. _____
7. _____
8. _____
9. _____
10. _____
11. _____
12. _____

Some women find they need to give up movie theaters, malls, some TV shows, and sometimes even a church or things they love, at least temporarily. Friends or family members involved in a husband's addiction may need to be avoided, at least for a season, and perhaps forever. Without these needed boundaries, we can continue to experience triggering that prohibits our healing.

But even with good boundaries around known triggers, there remains the chance that unexpected triggers may surprise us, catching us completely off guard. So let's focus on surprise triggers and how to deal with them.

## Planning for Surprise Triggers

Surprise triggers can come out of nowhere. My biggest emotional train wrecks have been by-products of surprise triggers. If you have a history of dissociation, as I do, the biggest challenge is blocking the automatic-dissociation-response that can kick in when a surprise trigger is suddenly in your space and overwhelms your capacity to remain grounded, because you didn't see it coming. A daily pursuit of continual self-awareness seems to be our only recourse.

Surprise triggers become much easier to navigate if you are still with your partner, and *if* he wants to be an ally in your healing. If he does, he can partner with you and help pre-plan for unexpected triggers. If you team, he can take over and navigate you both through surprise triggers when they suddenly appear. Couples often pre-choose a "code" word that they will use to signal each other that a trigger has appeared. That's a sign they need to leave, or he needs to manage the situation in a way that protects his wife.

But we *all* need to be prepared to manage triggers alone, because at times we will be alone when they strike. I suggest you always have taxi phone numbers and fare; a predetermined list of support women you can call; money for a hotel, should you need to not go home; and anything else that can help you do good self-care when you are slammed by panic.

During a group session, one woman shared a creative way she has pre-thought triggers and how she cares for herself when they come. She wrote the following on a card she carries in her purse:

> (Name), if you are not feeling safe...
> You can leave the movie anytime you want.
> You can leave the restaurant anytime you want.
> You can leave the party anytime you want.
> You can leave the meeting anytime you want.
> You can leave the hotel anytime you want.
>
> "I carry it in my purse," she adds, "and anytime my fingers graze it there, it is a visceral reminder—a body memory—that I have a VOICE. After all the times I have frozen, and sometimes still do, it is a helpful reminder."

I suggest you write this woman's list on a 3x5 or larger card and laminate it so it will last and be easy to find in your purse. I wish I had thought to do this list when I was still married, because there were times when such a card could have made a huge difference in how I responded in triggering situations. I know this exercise will help empower you when those painful surprise triggers come in your life.

## How I Will Deal with Surprise Triggers

1. _____
2. _____
3. _____
4. _____
5. _____

## Boundaries We Set to Limit Others' Impact on Us

What kind of boundaries do you have with the sex addict in your life?

_____
_____
_____
_____

In part two of this chapter, we'll learn the how-to's of creating healthy boundaries, especially with our partner. But in general, boundaries are about taking responsibility for ourselves and our lives—not about controlling others. However, even self-care boundaries we impose on ourselves will affect those close to us. And those boundaries may be interpreted as abandonment or control, even if our only motive is to take responsibility for ourselves and our healing. Perhaps an unrelated example will help you understand how healthy limits/boundaries can complicate relationships, especially in relationships where we have formerly had few boundaries:

> **Example:** *If you needed to keep the next-door neighbors' children's baseball from breaking your window, you would not erect a fence on their property to keep the ball out of your yard. Doing so would be trespassing. Instead, you would build a fence on your property to protect your home from fly balls. Even so, your neighbor may feel shunned because she can no longer interact with you when you're both in your backyards. Though your intention would not be to damage your friendship, your neighbor may perceive it that way.*

Likewise, if you need for your husband to sleep in a separate room temporarily to give your mind and body space and time to recover, he may feel banished, abandoned, and perhaps even punished. But your intention is to build emotional safety and privacy *around yourself so you are able to sleep.* Without the ability to feel safe enough to sleep, healing alludes you—and so does the healing of your marriage. The key is to keep your spirit soft toward him. If you can do that, hopefully he will recognize your need to heal is simply a natural outcome of his betrayal, and your need is likely only temporary.

## Sexual Boundaries

Do you need to draw a temporary sexual boundary around yourself to allow yourself time to heal before resuming sexual activity? Many women find they need a separate bedroom for a time. A few need their husbands to temporarily live elsewhere so they can create enough peace and calm in their homes to begin to heal.

It's important for you to know that a period of sexual abstinence is not inappropriate. Many couples impacted by sex addiction set aside a period of 30, 60, or 90 days of sexual abstinence to allow for mental, emotional, and relational healing. This time can help the addict reprogram his thinking before resuming sexual activity with his wife. Many men find they need to do this to let go of the fantasy life they engaged in prior to entering recovery. A period of "mental housecleaning" is often recommended to help the two of you genuinely reconnect without ghosts from his addiction.

On the other hand, if you feel a strong need to reconnect with your husband sexually, that is okay, too. Many counselors who specialize in sexual addiction tell our husbands they need to meet our physical desire to express our love sexually, if indeed we feel that need. However, husbands need to do this with honor, which means without images from their past. And that can be difficult in early recovery without a period of abstinence. Ideally, as you learn to detach and let go to allow your husband to work on his recovery, and you to work on yours, you will be able to tolerate a time of sexual abstinence, if he needs it. Just as we need boundaries in some areas in order to make room for our healing, sex addicts very often need a sexual timeout to clean their minds before reconnecting physically with their wives.

As you consider your sexual relationship with your husband, are there changes that need to be made? Do you need to erect sexual boundaries of some kind? If so, what are those changes? Since this is a very private matter, you won't be asked to share your answers to this question in your group, unless you request a discussion on sexual boundaries.

_____
_____
_____
_____
_____
_____
_____

## Sexual Addiction Recovery and Boundaries

Your husband has violated your vows and your trust, shattering your reality with betrayal trauma. But you love him, and he says he is willing to do whatever it takes to heal the marriage. How can you feel safe enough to stay to see if he will change?

While you are powerless to control your husband and his recovery, and you should not dictate your husband's sexual addiction recovery program, it is your responsibility to determine what you need in order to feel safe staying in your relationship for a period of time, while giving him time to "do" recovery

Though not every sex addict's program is exactly the same, there is a common list that most specialists recommend sex addicts include in their recovery efforts. As the wife of a sex addict, that list is important to you because the survival of your marriage—and possibly your physical health—depend on the quality of your husband's recovery efforts. In a way, the effort he puts into his recovery program is a kind of insurance policy for your marriage and family. Loving a sex addict presents a huge risk, as you've already learned. And if you take that risk, you'll need an insurance policy.

## Common Basic Sex Addiction Recovery Elements

1. **A mental health evaluation:** Because many people who struggle with addiction of any kind also have untreated mental health issues, such as depression, ADHD, anxiety, or others, it is wise for a sex addict to see a trained professional for a mental health evaluation. And if issues present themselves, to be treated for them. This step nearly always helps an addict be more successful in his recovery efforts. ADHD in particular presents in a high percentage of sexual addicts, and medication can be helpful.

2. **Attending Sex Addiction Anonymous or comparable meetings:** These 12 step meetings provide support, accountability, safety, a place and content to use for growth, "fellowship," and more. And for men who have a hard time

being emotionally intimate with their partners—and many sex addicts do—the fellowship of a good 12 step group provides a way to learn to "be real" about what they are thinking, feeling, and struggling with. And that kind of transparency is a stepping stone to learning how to "do" emotional intimacy in their marital relationships.

3. **"Work" the 12 Steps with a sponsor:** "Working the 12 steps" requires reading 12 step literature, doing written exercises that help one apply the steps to life, and meeting weekly with a sponsor to go over written work and gain encouragement and direction in recovery. Going to meetings without working the steps won't produce much change. *It's the process of working those steps with a good sponsor that eventually works them into our souls.*

4. **Meeting with a therapist if there are issues to be worked on:** Not every sex addict has childhood issues that need to be healed, or other issues in their lives that fuel their addiction, but most do. If that's your husband's case, counseling with a CSAT or other therapist trained in working with sex addicts will be an important part of his program. Because many addicts have used sexual stimulation as their "drug of choice" to deal with emotional pain or anger, healing those underlying issues that help fuel the addiction is extremely important for long term sobriety.

## Changes You Can Expect to See as He Grows in His Recovery

As a sex addict grows in his recovery process, changes in attitude toward his wife, and other new behaviors begin to appear. These include

- A softening and new gentleness toward you.
- An effort to guard his eyes, mind, and heart from things that trigger addictive thoughts.
- Working to protect and nurture your marriage and family.
- A growing responsibility with finances.
- Honoring commitments at work, in recovery, and at home.
- Growing honesty that replaces his habit of lying.

But this kind of new growth doesn't usually begin to appear for months into a solid, committed recovery program, especially if an addict's heart has grown hard before discovery. As you strive to wait for the fruits of his heartfelt change, use all the tools you're learning. Detachment, self-care, boundaries, taking responsibility for your own joy and life, and your own support and healing network can help you hang in there as you wait. Hopefully, within a year, you will begin to reap the benefits noted in the bullet list above. But remember, true change takes time, so patience on the front end is required.

Depending on where your husband is in recovery, this exercise can be encouraging or unsettling.

Do you see your husband taking responsibility for his recovery? What recovery behaviors do you—or don't you—see in his life at this time? Are there areas you need to discuss with him? If so, list them here. But hold off talking to him about them until we've had time to work through the remainder of this chapter together, so you can share your concerns with him in the most helpful way possible.

_____
_____
_____
_____
_____
_____
_____

## Tasks, Tools & Truths Discussed in Part 1 of this Chapter

1. Boundaries are the key to our empowerment.
2. Our boundaries develop out of our life experience.
3. Boundaries are an important aspect of self-care.
4. Boundaries are crucial to helping us deal with triggers.
5. Boundaries enable us to care for ourselves in relationships.
6. Boundaries enable us to pre-determine our sexual boundaries.
7. Boundaries enable us to evaluate our safety in a relationship with a sex addict, by observing the addict's recover in action.

## APPLICATION: APPLYING TRUTH TO LIFE

From my work in this section I realize that I need to take the following action steps:

_____
_____
_____
_____
_____
_____
_____
_____
_____
_____

# Boundaries: Part II

## Crafting & Using Boundaries Wisely

Now that we've talked about how boundaries can help us care for ourselves and heal, and what they can do for our relationships, let's roll up our sleeves and talk about how to craft healthy boundaries.

## A Helpful Boundaries Formula

There is a little boundaries formula therapists often teach their clients to help them learn how to create their own boundaries. It's short, easy to remember, and once you get it, it's easy to use:

> *When you* (insert the other person's behavior) *I make up* (the "story" you read into the other person's behavior). *And in response I feel* (insert the emotion you feel in response to what you make up). *Would you be willing to* (insert the specific change of behavior you need to see) *so* (the outcome you need in the situation)?

## A Boundaries Scenario

To gain understanding of how this formula works, let's take a scenario that might happen to anyone married to a sex addict. Then we'll apply the boundaries formula to that situation in order to learn how to create a boundary in any scenario between you and your husband, or you and anyone else.

In our scenario, it's late afternoon. You are in the kitchen preparing dinner, when your husband bursts through the garage door, rushes through the kitchen, and heads straight to the bathroom, closing the door behind him. Because he's previously agreed not to take his cell phone into the bathroom with him, and this time he didn't lay it on the kitchen counter as he agreed to do and always does—and didn't even stop and kiss you on the check on his way through the kitchen—alarm sirens begin to scream in your head. And the hot flush of a trigger rises in your body, increasing your heart rate and making it hard to concentrate on what you're cooking. **Without even meaning to, you "made up" a story about what he's up to. And objectivity was lost.**

*From Betrayal Trauma to Healing & Joy*

## Identify the Story You Make Up That Generates Your Feelings

The "making up a story" is generally a subconscious step. We don't even realize we do it. As a partner of a sex addict, your reality has been so "messed with" by the gaslighting addict in our life that it's often difficult to know what is real and what isn't. And because his rush-through-the-kitchen-without-laying-his-phone-on-the-counter is a trigger for you, rationally observing your thoughts and feelings to determine the reality about what's going on proves extra challenging—or impossible. Triggers do that to people!

Did he rush through and forget to lay his phone on the counter because he ate something at lunch that has his stomach churning? Or did he rush through intentionally taking his phone with him because he just got a Facebook message from an old girlfriend that he can't wait to read it?

It's interesting to consider how our minds (and wounded hearts) can color a situation without us consciously realizing that's what we're doing.

In the scenario above, what story might you "make up" or how might you interpret his actions?

_____
_____
_____
_____

## Just the Facts, Ma'am, Just the Facts

But if we can take a step back emotionally and observe *only* his actions without passing judgment on his actions, we can gain objectivity. As a practice exercise, reread the scenario above, then write down what your husband did without passing judgment on his actions. It will sound something like, "I saw my husband rush through the kitchen without saying, "Hi," and he took his phone into the bathroom with him."

_____
_____
_____
_____

As you can see, when we don't add our emotions to a situation, we simply report the facts; the black and white reality we observed.

But because you are wounded, and it's early in your healing journey, dissecting reality in a heated moment without passing judgment, or "making up" a story, is extremely difficult. If we "make up" that his actions have something to do with his addiction, we may go to the bathroom door, bang on it and shout: "Open the door! I know you're in there with your phone! You promised not to take it to there with you, and now you've broken your promise! I knew I couldn't trust you!"

On the other hand, if you make up that he might be sick, you may go to the bathroom door and say, "Honey, are you okay? Do you need help with anything?" *How we subconsciously interpret a situation dictates how we will experience and respond to it.*

So a big step in learning healthy boundaries involves forcing ourselves to stop and consciously think about what we can actually see, hear, smell, touch, and observe. Learning to think rationally about what happens in our relationships, before we react based on a false reality made up by our hurt and triggers, is the first empowering step in learning how to craft healthy boundaries. While we cannot know why he rushed through the kitchen—phone in hand—until he tells us, we do have the power to choose how to think about why he did it until we have more information. And growing in this way is not only empowering, it also de-escalates interactions that could otherwise make your home a very difficult place to live, and delay or prevent healing.

## Identify Your Needs & the Outcome You Desire in the Scenario

Before we can ask for what we need in the form of a boundary request, (1) we must know what we need in a specific situation, and (2) we must know the outcome we desire in the situation. Without knowing these two things, it's impossible to formulate good boundary requests.

In chapter one of this workbook we said that learning to ask ourselves, "What do I need right now?" is important in our healing process. It's impossible to do good self-care if we don't know what we need. And identifying our needs is important in crafting boundaries because when we feel emotional pain, it usually means at least one of our needs is not being met. Therefore, part of having healthy boundaries is learning to ask for what we need in specific situations.

If you picture yourself in our make-believe scenario with your husband and his phone in the bathroom, what would be your two or three greatest needs? Truth? Safety? Respect for your boundaries? Understanding from him about how his actions feel to you? Information about what he is doing in there?

_____
_____
_____
_____
_____

*From Betrayal Trauma to Healing & Joy*

Taking your needs into consideration, what outcome do you want in this dilemma? What actions from him could meet your needs and produce the outcome that will help you heal?

_____
_____
_____
_____

I have inserted my need and my desired outcome into the boundaries formula below to help demonstrate how your needs and the outcome you desire fit into learning to use the boundaries formula to create healthy boundaries:

> *When you* (take your phone in the bathroom) *I make up* (that you are going back to your addictive behavior). *In response I feel* (terrified and at risk). *Would you be willing to* (MARSHA'S NEED: eliminate triggering surprises in the future when you can OUTCOME MARSHA DESIRES: by calling me in advance to let me know what to expect when you get home?)

Now you put it all together and give it a try:

> *When you take your phone in the bathroom*
> *I make up* _____ .
> *And in response I feel* _____.
> *Would you be willing to* _____
> *so I can* _____?

By taking the time to think about it and write it down before making a boundary request, you are better prepared to ask for what you need in a healthy way, which in turn creates opportunity for your husband to understand you and try to meet your needs, if he thinks he can or wants to.

**IMPORTANT NOTE:** When we communicate with ourselves (in our thoughts), or with others, most of us struggle to tell the difference between a thought and a feeling. And knowing the difference is critical to healthy, fair boundaries. A feeling is *always* an emotion and it always comes from inside you. Two big mistakes most of us make, unless we work hard not to, include:

- **OWNING OUR FEELINGS**
- **STAYING OUT OF OTHER PEOPLE'S HEADS**

**EXAMPLE:**

1. Not owning a feeling, and leaving out an emotion: "I feel like you don't understand me." In this sentence the word "feel" is a verb, not a feeling. And

"you don't understand me" is a <u>judgement about what's going on in someone else's head</u>. And this communication is destined to fail.

When we talk about our feelings, we are talking about *our emotions, such as fear, joy, disgust, anger. And we are taking responsibility for those emotions, not blaming another for creating them in us.*

Let's try it following the rules above:

"I feel afraid, because I don't know if you understand me." In this sentence you bravely label your emotion, and you own your concern and recognize it is coming from inside you. And the healthy, logical next step is to ask a question so you can know whether or not you are understood.

"I feel <u>afraid</u> because I don't know if you understand me. I've written down my needs; would you be willing to read them, then talk about them together in a counseling session, please?" (Or alone, if your communication with your partner is healthy enough to tackle it alone.

**NOTES ABOUT NEEDS:** Like feelings, needs are about *you*. "I need you to stop_____" is not a need. Needs are about you, and they require vulnerability, which can feel scary when you are with a sex addict in early recovery.

Needs partners of sex addicts typically voice include things like safety; time to grieve; support; times for fun; meetings; space from the one who has betrayed them; financial security, etc.

## Putting It to Use in Real Life

Try your hand at using the formula by thinking of a real or potential scenario in your marriage, either past or present. Then use the boundaries formula to think through and use each of the formula's steps. Until this becomes second nature, I encourage you to actually type or write the formula, then fill in the blanks for each boundary situation that comes up in your life. It's guaranteed to help prevent relational train wrecks, and the skill becomes your own more rapidly if you use your body (hands and eyes) to write out the boundary request.

*When you* _____
*I make up* _____,
*And in response I feel* _____.
*Would you be willing to* _____
*so* _____ ?

*From Betrayal Trauma to Healing & Joy*

## But We Must Accept That the Outcome Is Out of Our Hands

It would be lovely if relationships and conflicts were always as easy as using the little boundaries formula above, and voila! Our needs would be met. However, there are many things in life and in relationships that we want, but we lack the power to bring them about *because we cannot control other people*. So even if we learn to use the formula above faithfully, the one we are asking may need to, or want to, say no.

In other situations, we may be able to achieve our desired outcome if we secure help. For instance, if your partner isn't yet in recovery, and you need to confront him about his addiction and request change, doing it on your own will likely fail. However, if you have a friend in recovery who will help you, confronting your husband with your friend's help increases the odds that your husband will listen, and perhaps even get into recovery. But what happens when the other person says no to a boundary request, and getting help won't change his mind?

## Determining Your "Deal Breakers"

Knowing what we need (and what we can and cannot live with or without) is an important part of having healthy boundaries and growing healthy relationships. It's also an important part of self-awareness and self-care. Some needs are so important to us that they are "deal breakers," meaning if a need is not met, we will leave the relationship.

Though our deal breakers are uniquely our own, things like monogamy, honesty, a rigorous recovery program, and access to household income and records appear on most partner's lists. These are black and white, make or break needs. Deal breakers. And in those situations, your action step is clear, though it's far from easy.

On the other hand, if you are not willing to lose a relationship over your need, it's time to consider alternate ways to meet your need yourself if the other person can't help meet your need by accepting your boundary.

Gratefully, our practice bathroom scenario is likely not a deal breaker for you, and you probably have the power to verbalize your need with fairly good results. But in each boundary you consider setting, ask yourself:

- Do I have the power in this relationship to produce good results if I ask that this need be met?
- Do I need help, and if I do, is there someone in my life who understands sex addiction and can help me, and potentially get positive results?
- Or am I powerless in this situation because the one with whom I need to draw a boundary does not see the circumstance the way I do?
- And if I am powerless, can I live with this unmet need, or meet it in some other way? Or is it so important to me I will have to leave the relationship if he or she won't meet my need?

Your answers to the following boundaries questions help you determine what action you want to take:

- Do you ask for what you need?
- Do you get help in making your request?
- Do you ask for what you need, knowing that need may not be met, then let your need go—or meet it in another way—if the one you ask won't, or can't, meet it?

And if your request is rejected, can you live with this unmet need, or meet it in some other way? Or is it so important to you that you will have to leave the relationship if he or she won't meet your need?

Or do you *not* even ask, but instead let that need go and find alternate ways to take care of yourself. In these difficult questions, we need to be aware that resentment can grow and build in us if we live with an unmet, ongoing need. And it's our responsibility to either not let that happen, or to free the other from the relationship if our resentment continues inside us.

## Utilizing the Paradox of Powerlessness vs. Empowerment

### Recognizing & Accepting Our Powerlessness

Just as the 12 steps tell us, we are powerless over other people. We must face the fact that our boundaries may be ignored. And if our partner's sobriety is what we're after, even if we lock our partners in our homes, we cannot control what goes on in their minds. They are, by God's design, beyond our control. We may draw healthy boundaries; we may nag and cry and scream. But in the end, we cannot control other people. Like it or not, we can ask for what we need; but unless the one we ask cares about our needs, we are truly powerless over their actions.

And when we do try to control, the consequences usually prove disastrous. Cloud and Townsend write:

> *If you are controlling your spouse's freedom and separateness, you are no longer an object of love. You have become two things that your spouse will rebel against because it is part of God's plan. You have become the master of a slave, and you have become a parent. A spouse was never intended to be either.*[20]

During a group session, as these principles sank in, one participant recognized the truths in this statement, and the lessons their words held for her. By overcompensating for her husband's lack of concern about his addiction, she suddenly realized she had participated in keeping them both stuck—where they had been for more than a decade. And as that truth dawned on her, she soberly spoke her thoughts out loud: "That means he will never grow up if I keep acting like his mother." How very, very true.

---

[20] Henry Cloud, PhD, John Townsend, PhD, *Boundaries in Marriage* (Grand Rapids: Zondervan, 2000). 104

From that moment on, she chose to (1) detach; (2) stop overcompensating for her husband in family matters; and (3) start making the needed life-changes to help herself and her children move forward, with or without him. Though she fully recognized her powerlessness over her husband, she refocused her energy on using her empowerment for her own healing and her children's well-being. Because this lagging-behind man loves his family, I think he will soon realize that if he wants to keep them in his life, it is time he becomes empowered and takes charge of his responsibilities and recovery. If he does, he will finally be ready to do sincere recovery work and change.

In what ways do you recognize your powerlessness to get your husband to do solid recovery if he isn't taking responsibility for himself? How do you feel about your husband's current recovery efforts?

_____
_____
_____
_____
_____
_____
_____

## Understanding & Stepping into Our Empowerment

Recognizing our powerlessness over the addict we love—and refocusing on our empowerment to care for ourselves, make changes in our own lives, and develop healthy boundaries—requires hard work and huge effort. But with it comes a new kind of freedom and power. I love group work because we learn best from each other. Listen to the wisdom in the words of women who have gone before you on this Journey:

- *I used to say, 'You can't do this,' or 'You can't do that,' and it drove him away. Now I realize I was trying to control him. But I'm beginning to see that boundaries and empowerment are all about me and what I need in my life so I can heal.*
- *I can make a trade. I can use the time I once used to monitor my husband and invest it my own healing and recovery. This will give him time to try real recovery, if he wants it, and opportunity for me to learn whether there is hope for our marriage. I realize I believed his sobriety was the key to my happiness. But seeing it that way kept me a victim. Now I am taking responsibility for my own happiness, and it's empowering.*

It's a hard pill to swallow, but once we've shared our boundary requests, the outcome to a specific situation is in the other person's hands. But even when our boundary requests are rejected, we can act with empowerment over our own lives.

## What Does It Mean to Be a Helpmate?

Even as we seek to surrender our desire to control his recovery, we must recognize God has placed us in a unique position in our partner's life. The Bible refers to that role as "helpmate." Because when married, we live in a committed relationship, we carry a responsibility to give our partner the opportunity to heal. Remember that addiction is bondage. Those caught up in it are trapped. Your husband may never have the courage and the incentive to do the grueling work freedom requires unless you step into the role of becoming his true helpmate. That role requires you to kindly, lovingly, set limits on what you will live with.  He may ultimately reject those limits and go his own way, but you will have done everything possible to offer him recovery without trying to fix or control him.

## Boundaries for the Journey

Each of our stories is different. Some among us will have the continued opportunity to grow in their ability to use boundaries in their marriages, as well as in other relationships. Others, like me, will need to practice and grow their skills with boundaries in other kinds of relationships. But however we do it, one of the most significant gifts we can give ourselves, those we love, and those we meet in life is learning, practicing, and applying healthy boundaries.

## Tasks, Tools & Truths Discussed in Part 2 of this Chapter

1. The boundaries formula and how to use it.
2. Recognizing and identifying the unconscious story we make up in our heads, and "unlearning" it.
3. Identifying the facts in the situation.
4. Identifying our need and desired outcome.
5. Owning our feelings.
6. Recognizing our powerlessness over others.
7. Determining our "deal breakers".
8. Understanding and stepping into our empowerment.
9. Understanding the concept of becoming a "helpmate", while accepting our powerlessness over others.

**APPLICATION: APPLYING TRUTH TO LIFE**

From my work in this section I realize that I need to take the following action steps:

_____
_____
_____
_____
_____
_____
_____
_____
_____
_____
_____
_____

Vicki Tidwell Palmer, LCSW, CSAT, has done a wonderful job in helping partners of sex addicts learn how to use her version of the formula in her very helpful book, *Moving Beyond Betrayal: The 5-Step Boundary Solution for Partners of Sex Addicts* (Central Recovery Press, 2016). If, after completing this chapter, you want further help and growth with boundaries, I heartily recommend getting a copy of Vicki's book and using it in a support group. A Circle of Joy offers "Effective Boundaries," a support group based on Vicki's book. Whether you study the book on your own, or in a group, I guarantee it will serve you well.

# 6

# Lost & Found: Finding Treasures in Your Trauma Chest

Whether your marriage has ended because of your husband's sexual activity, or you are still together, you've lost something because of his actions. In fact, you've probably lost *many* things, at least temporarily. Your loss is ongoing, and you are probably still grieving it. For one woman, the grieving process may take several months; for another, it may involve a few years. And for a few, the loss is so deep and long-lasting, they choose to leave the marriage. Unable to get over the loss they've experienced through betrayal, they now add the marriage to the list of losses.

Whatever you've lost, you now find yourself in a grieving process. Where do you think you are on the grieving continuum? To help you quantify your place in this process, use a scale of 1 to 100 to measure your healing. If 1 means you are still buried in grief and just beginning to process the loss, and 100 indicates full healing and readiness to move on, where do you currently fall on most days? Do you have any sense of how long it's going to take you to feel *"normal"* again?

_____
_____
_____
_____

Wherever you find yourself in grieving, it's important to allow yourself to mourn. But experts in loss and grief distinguish between healthy and unhealthy grief. "Normal" grieving begins to ease over time, and at some point in the process, you are able to function again. If you find over time you seem stuck in deep grief or anger, or if you can't access your feelings to drain them, seek help to identify why you are stuck. For those who can't seem to dislodge the pain through verbal expression and standard counseling, EMDR often proves helpful.

What have you lost? On the following list, mark the things you feel you've lost. If you think your loss is temporary, put a "T" by it. If you believe it is permanent, use a "P."

___Self-esteem    ___Innocence         ___Love            ___Home

___Meaning        ___Identity          ___Safety          ___Hope

___Direction      ___Shared friends    ___Best friend     ___Companionship

___Joy            ___Peace             ___Trust           ___Financial Security

___Family         ___Fun               ___Being a family  ___Your Youth

___In-laws                             ___Your self

___Health insurance                    ___Emotional security

___Connection with God                 ___Your support network

___The ability to be a stay-at-home mom    ___Time for leisure in your life

___Someone to help bear life's burdens     ___Your life as you know it

___A father for your children          ___Sexual relationship
___Happiness

_____         _____

_____         _____

Choose one loss, then to help process that loss in your life, answer the following questions about it. If you find it helpful to journal your answers to these questions this way, you can come back to them with other losses on your list. By journaling your answers to the questions regarding a loss, you can continue to do grief work as needed as you move toward healing.

**Loss #1:** _____

What feeling does this loss bring up in you?

_____
_____
_____
_____
_____
_____
_____
_____

Marsha Means, MA

Has this loss affected the way you function? If so, how?

_____
_____
_____
_____
_____

Has this loss affected your social life and/or your support system? If so, in what ways?

_____
_____
_____
_____
_____
_____
_____
_____

What is the most painful aspect of this loss?

_____
_____
_____
_____
_____
_____
_____

What do you especially miss because of this loss?

_____
_____
_____
_____
_____
_____
_____
_____
_____

*From Betrayal Trauma to Healing & Joy*

Perhaps you've experienced earlier losses in your life. Are any earlier losses being *hooked* by this loss? If so, in what ways?

_____
_____
_____
_____
_____
_____
_____
_____
_____

One of the most difficult losses many of us experience is the loss of our sense of self, *of who we are in our own eyes,* and our place in the world. Because as married women we often see ourselves as "Tom's wife," or as a one-half of our *coupleship* with our partner, we lose focus of who we are individually. When the connection with our partner is shattered by betrayal, we lose a big part of our identity. We can better understand this shift in self-perception as we recognize the trauma contained in betrayal.

"Trauma," Thomas Gerlach tells us, "is any experience that reduces who we are, or who we understand ourselves to be. The unregulated emotional intensity of the traumatic event reduces us to less than we were before it."

By its very nature, trauma reduces our sense of self because it reduces our empowerment—our ability to manage our lives and emotions, and stay on course. The traumatic event—whether it was a hurricane that swept away our house, or betrayal trauma that shattered our primary attachment—was *beyond our control to manage.* Therefore, we feel a sense of disempowerment.

Has this traumatic betrayal reduced you to less than you were before you discovered it? If so, in what ways?

_____
_____
_____
_____
_____
_____
_____
_____
_____

Has this traumatic betrayal *increased* your sense of self or strength in some way? If so, how?

___

Dealing with loss means reclaiming the parts of our lives that can be reclaimed, but it also means adjusting our lives to fit a new reality. Adjustment is internal, as well as external. Internally, we may need to see ourselves differently than we did before. Externally, we may need to find new social networks, support, employment, or perhaps a whole new life. What adjustments do you need to make? What adjustments have you made so far to accommodate the losses in your life?

___

The Life Model tells us that our joy strength has to be higher than our pain or we can't heal emotionally, even in therapy. And, as we've said before, the very best way to increase our joy strength is to connect with others at a heart level—sharing pain and experiencing love, understanding, and acceptance—as we are doing in this group. Sharing and support helps our brains reconnect to joy and allows the joy center to once again function. As it does, healing takes place. That's one reason why learning to keep our joy cups full, even as we heal, holds such importance in the healing process.

What other steps can you take to increase your joy strength by increasing joy bonds beyond the scope of this group? As we approach the end of this part of your healing process, what joy-based relationships do you already have in your life? Do you have enough, or do you need to find and build more?

___

What else might help plug the holes left by your losses? How can you keep your joy cup filled in ways that bring light back into your life?

___

## Finding Treasures in the Trauma Chest

Among their losses, many women also discover unexpected gifts. It's still early in your healing, but have you yet seen glimpses of gifts you could never have expected? Treasures buried deep in your traumatic loss? If so, what are they?

___

What role is your faith in God playing in this loss in your life? How can you maximize the potential many find in a relationship with God in order to maximize your healing?

_____
_____
_____
_____
_____

What have you learned about yourself through your loss?

_____
_____
_____
_____
_____
_____
_____
_____
_____
_____
_____
_____
_____

## Tasks, Tools & Truths Discussed in this Chapter

1. Betrayal trauma produces losses.
2. Trauma produces a loss of personal-power.
3. We lose our sense of self
4. Identifying and processing our losses.
5. Grieving our losses takes time.
6. Intentional joy can help us heal from the loss.
7. Loss requires life-adjustments to fit our new reality.
8. Most find some treasure as a result of the losses.
9. Loss produces growth.

## APPLICATION: APPLYING TRUTH TO LIFE

From my work in this chapter I realize I most need to work on...

_____
_____
_____
_____
_____
_____
_____
_____
_____
_____

# 7

# Finding Your Way Back to You

Discovering your husband is involved with any kind of inappropriate sexual activity—even mental activity—can shatter your self-esteem, leaving only a fragmented view of your worth. It can feel as if his actions are all about you, and that you are not good enough to satisfy him completely. Though in our heads we know he would struggle no matter who he was married to, in our hearts—and feminine egos—it may remain almost impossible to believe that truth.

Which of the lies listed below have you been tempted to believe because of your husband's behavior?

__ I'm not a lovable person

__ I'm not pretty enough

__ I'm not sexy enough

__ I'm not young enough

__ I must not have been spiritual enough

__ God doesn't care

__ I didn't give him sex often enough

__ I've lost myself

__ I'll be alone for the rest of my life

__ Life will never feel good again

__ At least he didn't have an affair

__ At least he didn't have sex with men

__ At least it wasn't child pornography

__ At least he didn't get arrested

__ _____

__ _____

Can you tell yourself that your husband's behavior had nothing to do with you and believe it at this point in your journey? Why, or why not?

_____
_____
_____
_____

*From Betrayal Trauma to Healing & Joy*

As women, it's almost as if our Creator designed us to "tuck under the arm" of the man we love—to settle into that seemingly safe, sheltered place, knowing we'll never again have to do life all alone. This feels especially true for women who marry young and spend decades with their husbands, seemingly protected from suffering life's storms alone.

But then the slow pulling away begins, and an aching loneliness settles in its place. Or the fateful day of discovery or disclosure crashes into our peaceful existence. And we realize our safe place is no more. Or perhaps it never existed at all. Like a lone woman dropped into a bombed-out, war-torn city, each of us is forced to find our way to help, to safety, and to some form of life on our own.

If you're still struggling to find your way *home* after the trauma and devastation of sexual addiction, we encourage you to keep going. There is a way back home—home to yourself, whether or not your marriage survives your personal holocaust. We hope this chapter will provide a map for part of that journey.

## Finding Your Voice, Speaking Your Truth

Many of us suffer this tragedy in silence, afraid that if we share our reality with people already in our lives, we and/or our husbands will be judged, rebuked, or cast aside like rotten garbage. While a lot of people are *not* safe enough to talk to, silent suffering is neither the answer in our individual lives, or in the world at large.

Silence is a strategy of the enemy of our souls and marriages. John 10:10 tells us, *"The thief"* [the enemy]*"comes to steal and destroy...."* And one way this thief steals and destroys is by shaming us into wearing masks of pretense, never finding safe places to share our reality with others who will care. He knows that with silence he can . . .

- Steal our stories
- Steal our healing
- Steal our joy
- Steal our dreams
- Steal our future
- Steal our life purpose

Sometimes he uses our husbands to silence us. Other times, he uses our ministers, our counselors, our families, or our friends.

Has fear or shame shushed you into silence? If so, who or what in your life has kept you quiet?

_____
_____
_____
_____

## Removing the Mask

I love a little story I read years ago, one I've since held close to my heart. It helped me learn how isolating and damaging my own pretense and mask-wearing had been in my life, and how much freedom and healing and joy awaits when we find safe places to share our truth. The story is about a vocalist named Tina.

Tina was the vocalist at a weekend women's retreat. Beautiful and poised, she wore a lovely, flattering dress and high-heeled shoes as she stood before her large audience. The story writer said she looked and sang just like an angel.

Following the last speaking presentation of the weekend, during which the speaker had shared the value of dropping our masks of pretense and getting real with one another, Tina sang her closing song. But as she hit the final, clear, penetrating notes, she reached up and grasped the front of her lovely, curly brown hair—and pulled it off her head! In her hand she held what the shocked audience suddenly realized was only a wig. The beautiful, angelic Tina quietly stood, mostly bare-headed, with sprouts of limp hair sticking up here and there. Looking down, she stepped out of her high heels and placed her feet directly on the carpet.

The large audience sat in stunned silence. Then suddenly, as if on cue, cheering women rose to their feet, clapping, weeping, overwhelmed—and grateful—for Tina's act of courage in their presence. When the crowd finally stopped clapping and quieted down, Tina shared that for many years she had suffered from trichotillomania, a compulsive hair-pulling disorder. Isolated and afraid, she hid her addiction because of the shame it brought.

The writer concludes:

> *Tina's acts freed something inside her. The secret she had covered for so many years was out in the open at last. God had given her the courage to reach down into the darkness of her addiction and lift it into the dazzling light of his love. Painful honesty and humility can set us free of our masks and our need to hide who we really are.*

What do you feel as you read Tina's story?

_____
_____
_____
_____
_____

*From Betrayal Trauma to Healing & Joy*

## The Power of Being Known

It's healing when someone knows us well enough to really see us as we are, yet accepts us anyway. If my friend knows me, and respects me as I do her, we become mirrors for one another. We reflect one another's value, helping each other see what we cannot see for ourselves, especially if we carry shame. This kind of intimate, healing connection can also help meet our leftover, unmet attachment needs from childhood, enabling us to develop new, healthy attachment bonds well into adulthood.

Who in your life really knows you yet loves you anyway? Think in terms of people who are there, or will be there, long term. If currently you have no one, at the end of this chapter we'll share ideas about how to find these safe people.

_____
_____
_____
_____
_____

What fears or which individuals make it unsafe for you to remove your mask at this time?

_____
_____
_____
_____
_____

Society has taught us we must seek to be beautiful and have it all together to be acceptable—to be loved and desired by a man. So we strive to measure up, always falling short because a fresh crop of young beauties emerges each spring. And as they do, we continue to age.

For those of us who didn't get what we needed from caregivers in early childhood, the knowledge that we are enough simply because we are unique creations of the Master Craftsman never crosses our minds. Instead, we continue to search our bathroom mirrors for a reflection that proves we measure up because we look good enough. We continue longing to be seen as ". . . separate and individual, to be loved for our uniqueness and ordinariness. To be accepted with our anxieties, our inevitable setbacks, our flaws."[21]

---

[21] Colette Dowling, *Perfect Women* (New York, NY: Simon & Schuster, 1988), 209.

Who in your life, if anyone, knows you this well and loves you anyway?

_____
_____
_____

## Finding—or Creating—Your Own Safe Place

In addition to reflecting your value and worth, a safe place can help you:

- Rekindle your joy.
- Reclaim your story
- Reframe your past
- Accept yourself, warts and all
- Strengthen the "I"
- Focus on your potential and consider your options
- Develop a plan
- Continue to heal and grow

## Rekindle Your Joy

Nothing extinguishes a woman's joy in life faster than discovering her husband is a sexual addict. Like a death sentence, it covers every facet of her world in gloom. How can we possibly rekindle our joy under those circumstances? If we are to survive, we must answer that question.

Proverbs 4:23 instructs us, *"Above all else, guard your heart, for it is the wellspring of life."* Just what is the "wellspring of life"? It is the place inside from which our joy flows, and life springs. Like a life-giving spring bubbling up from the forest floor high on a mountainside, joy is the elixir of life. Our Creator made us with brains that want to operate from joy. Just as a battery-powered toy will not run with a dead battery, neither can we heal or live reasonably happy lives without joy.

At its essence, joy is relational. Joy is generated by joy-producing relationships. We experience joy when someone we care about is glad to be with us. Joy produces warm, happy feelings—and we like it. Joy is the "belonging" we create around us as we reach out and connect at a heart level with others. In addition, joy bonds help heal trauma. No wonder it is the elixir of life.[22]

_____

[22] Jim Wilder, PhD, et. al., and Ed Khouri, MA, *The Life Model* (www.lifemodel.org).

What is your *joy factor* at this time? If 100 is "charged with joy," and 1 is "way down in the dumps," where are you on the joy scale this week?

_____
_____
_____
_____

If your joy factor is lagging, what action steps can you take to increase it?

_____
_____
_____
_____
_____

## Reclaim Your Story

"You are a story. You are not merely the possessor and teller of a number of stories; you are a well-written, intentional story that is authored by the greatest Writer of all time," author Dan Allender, PhD writes. ". . . The weight of those words, if you believe them, can change the trajectory of your life. . . . God shaped, molded, and formed us to reveal something about himself."[23]

Do you feel like a "well-written, intentional story" right now? What do you feel if you let yourself consider that God can somehow help you weave these dark chapters in your life story into a pattern that reveals something about God himself? Does that give you hope, or does it make you angry? Why?

_____
_____
_____
_____
_____

## Reframe Your Past

Dan goes on to say, "The story we are to live . . . doesn't truly begin until we face what we have lost and then turn to see the horizon of uncertainty ahead. Our story will gain momentum and depth only to the degree that we honestly embrace both loss and fear."[24]

---

[23] Dan Allender, PhD, *To Be Told* (Colorado Springs: Waterbrook Press, 2005), 11.
[24] Dan Allender, PhD, *To Be Told* (Colorado Springs: Waterbrook Press, 2005), 46.

To honestly embrace both loss and fear, we'll have to acknowledge all we've lost. And we'll have to keep detaching from our husbands' journey—or the loss of our relationship if that is our situation—over and over and over again, as many times as it takes. And as we do, we'll need to redirect our energy and work to change whatever we hold power to change in our own lives.

Where are you at this point in your efforts to embrace all you have lost and let it go?

_____
_____
_____
_____
_____

What fears remain in your life as you move ahead?

_____
_____
_____
_____

One group member reminded us that God cannot put something new in our hands if our fists are clenched. It takes an open-handed, palms-up attitude to readily receive whatever new joys and connections He has waiting for you. Are you ready to approach God and the future in an open-handed posture?

_____
_____
_____
_____

## Reframe Old Losses

If our self-esteem has been damaged by a husband's choices, part of changing a negative self-concept requires confronting painful messages and events from the past. If old wounds remain unhealed, we need to grieve them. If our needs remain unmet, we should find healthy ways to meet them. Many of us require a counselor's help to do this challenging work.

Have you already done your work to heal old life wounds? If not, has the time come to do it so you're ready to move toward new life? How might you begin that process?

_____
_____
_____
_____

Sometimes a poor view of ourselves is the result of mistakes we have made. Are there things in your past for which you need to forgive yourself before you can see yourself through God's loving and grace-giving eyes? If so, what are those things? *(This question is only for you; your answer need not be shared with anyone, unless you choose to share or ask for help in dealing with those things.)*

_____
_____
_____
_____

## Accept Yourself, Warts & All

For most of us in this beauty-crazed culture, accepting ourselves presents perhaps the hardest task of this journey. Yet it remains essential if we are to heal and move on in our lives. The little saying, "Welcome to the human race" may be glib, but it packs powerful wisdom. For we are human, fallible, and flawed.

But we are also creatures of the Creator's design. When God created you, He intentionally made you one of a kind. "No reprints, replicas, or reproductions. Each person would be an original, one of a kind, with the inherent worth of an original work of art crafted by the Master Craftsman."[25] His trademark is stamped on every heart. It's that hunger and craving for connection we feel, deep down in our souls.

Knowing this in our heads is the easy part; learning to live with grace and acceptance of what we see in the mirror proves much harder. Where are you in your ability to fix what you can fix, and accept what you cannot, resting in the belief that you are an original work of art?

_____
_____
_____

---

[25] Charles L. Whitfield, MD, *Healing the Child Within: Discovery and Recovery for Adult Children of Dysfunctional Families* (Deerfield Beach, FL: Health Communications, Inc. 1987).

If you have a ways to go toward accepting yourself, what do you think might help you make progress?

___

___

___

## Strengthen the "I"

Strengthening the "I," or intentionally developing a stronger, more clearly identified self, is one of the best ways to build a stronger marriage. I finally grasped this lesson during a week-long marriage intensive several years ago. Our skilled counselor taught us by using our entire bodies. To begin, he tossed three large floor pillows into a small triangle on the floor, placing them about 18 inches apart.

"Now," he said, "I would like each of you to stand in the center of your own pillow, hands at your sides, leaving the third pillow empty." With curiosity, we dutifully did as told.

"Your individual pillow and body represent you as an individual. Each of you is responsible for making your life work and for taking care of yourself. That," he told us, "is the primary task of adulthood."

He then asked us to each move one foot to the empty pillow. We were still anchored and grounded on our individual pillows, but we were now also sharing a third pillow.

"That," he admonished us, "represents what a healthy marriage looks like. In a healthy marriage, you don't take the other foot off your individual pillow and move both feet to the third pillow just because you choose to share your life with someone. You stay anchored in who you are and continue to function as a whole person, while sharing your life with your partner. Only "individuated," fully-functioning adults can choose to join another and become mutually interdependent. And mutual interdependence is essential for a healthy, growing marriage."

That real-life object lesson of what some therapists refer to as "the three-legged stool" of marriage helped me grasp that I am still responsible for me, even if I marry. And so is my partner. Neither of us now assumes responsibility for the other; nor do we surrender our selves fully to the *coupleship*. We will always be two separate people. Yes, there will be seasons of illness when one of us needs to carry the full load, or times when one must be away, leaving the other to keep the home fires burning. But all the while, two individuals continue to exist as they choose to share their lives. This synergistic partnership enriches the lives of both individuals.

*From Betrayal Trauma to Healing & Joy*

Each couple crafts their partnership differently. In one marriage, the husband may be the bread winner while the wife keeps their home and family running smoothly. In another, both partners may choose to work, then share responsibility for the family and the home. And in others, the wife works and the husband cares for the children and the home. In each of these partnerships, two healthy individuals come together synergistically.

Drs. John Cloud and Henry Townsend speak to this in their *Boundaries in Marriage* workbook:

> *We are responsible to each other, but not for each other. Spouses may help each other with the loads of life (the financial, health, or emotional crises that come along), but ultimately, each person must take care of his own daily responsibilities (including one's feelings, attitudes, values and handling of life's everyday difficulties.*[26]

What do you feel as you read this section on strengthening the "I"? What issues come to mind?

_____
_____
_____
_____
_____

How strong is your "I" at this time?

_____
_____
_____
_____
_____

How strong is your husband's "I"?

_____
_____
_____
_____
_____

---

[26] John Cloud, PhD, Henry Townsend, PhD, *Boundaries in Marriage Workbook* (Grand Rapids: Zondervan, 2000), 34.

Strengthening the "I" includes developing whatever interests, talents, or skills we possess to enrich our lives and gain the ability to manage life on our own, should the need arise. It means becoming fully adult so our husbands' wrong choices don't throw us into dependency, fear of financial destitution, or life-long enslavement to the emotional abuse of ongoing sexual addiction.

## Recognize & Focus on Your Potential & Consider Your Options

### *I Always, Always Have Choices*

Some among us have been groomed by the sexual addict and have learned to see ourselves as helpless in our situations. When this dynamic is at play in a relationship, it is termed "learned helplessness." Unrecognizable to us, this dynamic shapes us to see ourselves as victims of the sexual addict's choices. When we feel powerless and trapped, it may seem all routes to a healthier life are blocked.

But in truth, we always, always have choices. True, today's choices may not be the same as our end goal, but they *can* be stepping stones to the future we hope to create. And when we learn to recognize our choices and take them, they become windows of opportunity enabling us to build the life we want. Yes, it may take time; but life is a journey. As we're *becoming,* we can enjoy the trip.

We must determine the best course of action for our own lives and our children, especially if the one we love isn't interested in, or doesn't stay, in recovery. When we recognize opportunity and make the choice to take it, we usually feel hope and relief. We feel hope because now we know it is up to us. "No one else can take away their pain, give them happiness, or be held accountable for their successes or failures," writes the author of *Ordinary Women, Extraordinary Lives.* "By becoming willing to be responsible for themselves, they see that the only person who can solve their problems is the one looking back from the glass."

Author Colette Dowling adds, "Accepting responsibility for one's actions doesn't mean having to solve our problems alone. Support is essential. And most people know from the previous attempts that trying to make a change by oneself is difficult and disappointing. But now they can begin to look for help from nurturing friends and begin to build a network of support."[27]

By recognizing and making choices, we can take back our power, reclaim our stories, and take responsibility for our own happiness—even if the addict in our life isn't pursuing recovery.

Dr. Jennifer Schneider says this ". . . also means not waiting for his support—financially, emotionally, or in practical matters—for you to start your career, or change your career, or go back to school, or whatever it is you want do." She advises women to not think in

---

[27] Colette Dowling, *Perfect Women* (New York: Simon & Schuster, 1988), 9.

terms of needing his cooperation. Rather, ". . . make them (your decisions) as though you had no one but yourself on whom to lean." If you have areas you'd like to develop but you lack your husband's support, how might you begin to move toward that work without his help? Think baby steps, if necessary.

_____
_____
_____
_____

If you can't see possibilities at this time, do you need to find someone, or a group of women, to help you envision possibilities?

_____
_____
_____
_____
_____

God has gifted each of us with natural aptitudes and strengths. If those aptitudes aren't developed and functioning in our lives, we will feel frustration, boredom, or burn-out. When we discover, recognize, and hone these gifts from our Creator, we create more joy and life-satisfaction for ourselves and those around us. And with those things come a stronger sense of our God-given selves and some level of economic independence. This freedom enables us to take care of ourselves and our children alone, should that become necessary. In addition, it often earns us more respect in our husbands' eyes because they recognize we no longer have to stay in a destructive relationship. Husbands now see that we can survive without them. And sometimes, that becomes motivation for change.

Do you have natural aptitudes and strengths lying fallow that you would like to develop? What are they, and how might you take small steps to incorporate them into your future?

_____
_____
_____
_____
_____

## Develop a Plan

One of the most empowering things we can do to heal and move toward a life of hope and joy is to develop a plan, a sort of "What do I do now? Or what do I do if?" Many of us, especially those with young children, do feel optionless. As women, we know it's a 24/7 job to feed, shelter, and protect young children. Trying to consider the possibility of doing it all alone, *and earning a living*, overwhelms us. Yet for many, our circumstances reach a point that demands we find a way to make life work on our own. It's *much* better to be prepared than to discover we're stranded in a dark, dangerous alley with no way out.

Do you have a plan that will enable you to care for yourself and your children if your situation deteriorates and requires it? If not, what action steps can you take now to put one in place? Remember, your support structure can help you think this through and consider your options.

_____
_____
_____
_____
_____
_____
_____
_____
_____
_____
_____
_____

## Continue to Heal & Grow

Learning about our husband's sexual addiction throws us into a journey of loss. But it also introduces us to a time of transition that fosters growth, connection, and new life. William Bridges, author of a classic simply titled, *Transitions*, encourages:

*Find out what is waiting in the wings of your life. Whether you chose your change or not, there are un-lived potentialities within you, interests and talents that you have not yet explored. Transitions clear the ground for new growth. They drop the curtain so that the stage can be set for a new scene. What is it, at this point in your life that is waiting quietly backstage for an entrance cue? What new growth is ready to germinate in this season of your life?*

## Tasks, Tools & Truths Discussed in this Chapter

1. Recognizing and countering the lies.
2. Finding your voice and speaking your truth in safe places with safe people.
3. Learning the value of being "real".
4. Understanding the connection between safe people, joy, and healing.
5. Reclaiming your story.
6. Learning to "reframe".
7. Reaching self-acceptance.
8. Strengthening your "I".
9. Recognizing you have choices and developing a plan for safety and empowerment.

## APPLICATION: APPLYING TRUTH TO LIFE

From my work in this section, I realize I need to . . .

_____
_____
_____
_____
_____
_____
_____
_____
_____

## How to Find Other Women Going Through This Loss in Your Area

Finding safe women in your area going through pain and loss from a husband's sexual addiction might seem risky or even impossible. But with persistence, you'll learn you are from alone. Though these ideas will bear less fruit in rural areas or miles away from metropolitan areas, you will find others like you, no matter where you live. Here are some ideas others have tried with success.

## Basic Principles for Initial Anonymity

To keep your identity private, create a free email account to use only for these efforts and the contacts produced. If you plan to use the telephone in your search, consider carefully whether you want to use one of your own numbers. Another option, if you can afford it, is to use a prepaid cell phone, or one that only requires a small, month-by-month commitment. For individuals with a smart phone or a computer with Internet access, other possibilities include setting up a free Google Voice account that calls from a remote number or communicating via Skype, using a Skype name created only for this purpose.

If anonymity is important to you, consider a temporary post office box for contacting others and receiving mail through the postal service.

## Who to Contact

Anyone or any organization that helps meet the spiritual, emotional, social, or physical needs of local citizens can assist you in your search. Don't exclude men's groups. For every married man who struggles with sexual addiction, there's a wife who needs to connect. Though no one can legally give specific information about clients, those in helping professions can become a vital link if they make fliers you create available to those they serve.

Make your information available to—

- Ministers, priests, rabbis, women's ministry leaders, men's ministry leaders, and marriage ministry leaders.
- Support groups such as Divorce Care, Grief Care, Stephen's Ministries, Celebrate Recovery and similar church-related small groups where members may deal with this issue.
- Counselors and mental health professionals nearly always have clients dealing with sexual addiction, either the addicts themselves or spouses.
- Family law attorneys.
- Support groups through hospitals, the crisis line in your area, and any other social agency with a staff or groups who seek to empower women

- or help citizens deal with grief, loss, and major life transitions. Any and all of these may be in touch with women who need to connect and heal.
- Women's resource centers at area junior colleges and universities. Though they may go by slightly different names, these centers help women move toward empowerment and independence. Often, women use these resource centers because of failed marriages. Partners of sexual addicts are among them.
- Public libraries and area food banks. Both places may allow you to leave fliers or post one on a bulletin board. Any woman who has young children and is now struggling on her own to hold her family together is a likely recipient of food banks services.

## *How to Contact*

To compile a potential list of organizations, start with your local telephone directory or a search engine online. If you live in the United States, public libraries house area phone books in the reference section. Look for possible organizations under "Government Services" and in the yellow pages under "Counselors," etc.

Once you have a list, consider the best way to make contact. We suggest you begin with whatever feels safest and most comfortable to you. After gaining confidence, you can try other means.

Consider email, telephone calls/voice mail, or a short letter or flier through postal mail. Ask if you can leave fliers in agency offices, on church vestibule tables, in counselors' and doctors' waiting rooms, and any other place a woman might pick one up and tuck it in her purse.

However you begin, you may need persistence. It may require making more than one effort or attempt. Most organizations are overwhelmed with needs and understaffed to meet them. If you aren't worried about anonymity, nothing connects like a personal, face-to-face, brief meeting that includes a smile and a warm handshake.

If you can present yourself as someone available to help these groups assist some of the women they serve, you may feel more empowered. And if people sense that in you, they may be more responsive to your efforts.

## *Where to Meet with Other Women When You Find Them*

Consider this carefully. While nothing feels as personal as someone's living room, we know this topic holds the potential to flush out strangers with less than good motives. For that reason, public places are much safer.

If you initially meet each woman individually, choose to meet at a restaurant or café for tea or coffee. Select an establishment that offers enough space between patrons to maintain privacy.

As you move toward structured group meetings, consider available public places in your area. Libraries, as well as most hospitals, usually have public meeting rooms that can be reserved. Churches often open a room to support groups for a small monthly rental fee.

Finding a meeting place might require some work; but in the end, you will be grateful you invested the time. Remember you are worth the effort it takes to build a supportive group of women to walk alongside one other and heal together.

# 8

# Looking Ahead: Forgiveness, Trust & Beginning Again

*Every time you forgive, the universe changes.... —The Shack*

## Considering Forgiveness

Although forgiveness may seem far away in the distant future, at some point each of us needs to consider forgiving our partner for the pain and loss his actions have caused. Without forgiveness, the hurt in our heart plants the destructive seeds of resentment and bitterness. And when resentment and bitterness sprout in our heart, they not only wrap their roots around our marital relationships, they twist our very nature and interfere with all relationships. Over time, their grip even reshapes our countenance.

In a very real sense, forgiveness is something we do for ourselves. And it comes with a bonus: when we forgive, we create the opportunity for a happier future, whether we spend it alone, with our present husband, or someone new altogether

But how in the world do we get there? Before we try to answer that question, let's first look at what forgiveness is *not*.

## Forgiveness Is Not Forgetting

Author Linda Strom, who grew up with terrible abuse and now ministers in prisons, reminds us that we don't have to forget in order to forgive. "Forgiveness is not denying, ignoring or forgetting what we experienced or how we feel," she writes. "In spite of our best efforts to forget what we've done to others or what others have done to us, we can't forget the past. Our minds are greater than any computer and have an excellent, but usually unforgiving, memory."[28]

Yes, the memories will likely remain. But they will lose their sting and no longer hurt when they come to mind. Instead, they'll simply become a part of your personal story once you've fully processed them to resolution. Although processing memories may

---

[28] Linda Strom, *Karla Faye Tucker: Set Free* (Colorado Springs: Waterbrook Press, 2006), 55.

require EMDR or Immanuel Approach[29] therapeutic sessions to reach the resting point of resolution, it is possible.

## Forgiveness Doesn't Equal Trust

No, forgiveness does not equal trust; nor are we ever required to trust the one we forgive. Trust is something your husband will need to earn, slowly, over time, as you see "buy-in" and ongoing consistency in his recovery journey. We'll talk more about trust later.

## Forgiveness Doesn't Necessarily Mean Reconciliation

Nor does forgiveness mean reconciliation. Many of our husbands walk away, still choosing to live in addiction, never seeking repentance or offering amends. And some of us choose to walk away. If forgiveness required reconciliation, we would be held in bondage by the addict's choices, unable to heal, forgive, and move on.

### Can We Forgive and Remain Detached?

Absolutely! In many cases, we *must* remain detached because the addict hasn't yet demonstrated true heart-change, and it would be unsafe to reconnect emotionally with him. But his lack of change does not rob you of the freedom to forgive when you're ready to take that step for your own well-being.

## How Do We Make Forgiveness Happen?

Like everything else about this healing journey, forgiveness is a process. And it arrives differently for each of us. For a very few, forgiveness is almost immediate. Others need much more time. And some struggle for years to find the *release button* inside their hearts that will enable them to authentically surrender and take the forgiveness step.

### *Try Reframing*

Try *reframing* forgiveness as "changing the story of my life." Often, reframing a situation or a circumstance empowers us to see something from a different perspective. Our lives consist of the results of choices we make, so what we choose is very important. *Choosing* forgiveness gives you the opportunity to create a different future than you would otherwise have. Choosing forgiveness allows you to become a woman filled with peace.

If forgiveness still challenges you, as you answer the question below, do a second step and write (on a separate piece of paper) the things you still can't forgive. Then put the list in your God box. When we can't, in time, God can. In time, your heart will begin to soften and change.

---

[29] Karl Lehman, M.D., *Outsmarting Yourself: Catching Your Past Invading the Present and What to Do About It* (Libertyville, IL: The Joy! Books, 2011).

List the things your husband has done that you haven't yet been able to completely forgive.

___

What do you think is blocking your ability to forgive these particular things?

___

How often do these things come to mind?

___

How do you feel physically, emotionally, and spiritually when those thoughts surface?

___

How might it change your life to be able to completely forgive your partner?

___

How might it change your autobiography or your eulogy?

_____
_____
_____
_____
_____

### *Consider Forgiving One Event at a Time*

Some women find it easier to forgive one action or event at a time. It might prove beneficial to make a list, so you can see the individual events that block you. Then begin having ordinary conversations with God, talking about each item on the list. Let Him know how it hurts. Ask God for His help. Tell Him you are blocked from forgiveness, and remind Him it's His job—only He can enable you to experience enough heart-change around these hurts to release them.

One beautiful, spring day I received a note from a former support group member who labored over how to forgive her husband. Her hurt was so deep and terribly painful that I wondered if forgiveness would ever come for her. She desperately wanted to be free from her pain, and she wanted that freedom for her husband as well. He was working hard at recovery and was truly a changed man. When her support group ended, I asked her to email me when that day finally arrived so I could enjoy it secondhand.

As I read her words, tears filled my eyes and my heart felt overwhelming joy for her—and for her husband.

Her note simply said:

> Hi Marsha,
>
> *I was in a support group with you last year. You told me that you wanted me to send you an email when I was finally able to forgive. Well, forgiveness came today. It was healing for both of us. I felt a release and I felt tension leave my body the moment I said, "I forgive you."*
> *I am still in recovery and have come a long way.*
>
> *Mary*

I love it when this happens. It's the miracle of rebirth in broken hearts and lives, and the rebirth of a decades-long marriage after severe damage from sex addiction and betrayal trauma. Miracles such as these keep my hope alive.

If you've already been able to completely forgive your husband, what enabled you to do so?

_____
_____
_____
_____

### *Talk to God About It*

If you are still struggling with forgiveness in general, talk to God about it. We know our ability to forgive comes through Him. Our human nature feels entitled to hang on to past pain, and to require the one who hurt us to pay for his actions. Use the space below to talk to God about your struggle to completely let go of what your partner has done to hurt you. Remember, God already knows. But putting your thoughts and feelings down on paper and staying in daily dialogue with Him helps begin the change process in you, so that one day, like Mary, you can be free.

Dear God,

_____
_____
_____
_____
_____
_____
_____

## What About Trust?

It may be hard for you to imagine ever trusting your husband again. And if you have lost your marriage, you probably have difficulty imagining ever trusting some new man. I admit that I do. You know too much now. Your innocence has evaporated, along with fairy tales and childhood visions. And heart spaces once occupied by dreams now host reticence and self-protection.

Fear may break through only occasionally, now that you've processed many memories and much of the pain. Yet, as you face the future—even the present on the hardest of days—you must admit: fear still flutters deep in the hollows of your heart.

Trust is something that must be earned. This means, for the most part, we're powerless to produce it. Trust can only be generated by the sexual addict's choices. For that reason, addiction specialists caution us to "believe behavior, not words." It's easy for a sexual addict to say he's consistent and sober if words are all that's needed. But a softening and a new vulnerability with you are heart changes that indicate real change is likely happening. Getting to trust requires vulnerability on both partners' parts.

## Vulnerability: Sea Turtle or Slug?

*Vulnerability.* The very word sounds scary to a wounded heart. And frankly, if your husband is not pursuing rigorous recovery, allowing yourself to be vulnerable with him is not only scary, it's unhealthy. But if he is pursuing recovery, and if intimacy is going to be restored, eventually you much take the risk vulnerability requires. When I think of vulnerability, my mind envisions slugs and turtles. Have you ever thought about how vulnerable a slug is in the world?

I lived for years in the misty Northwest and grew accustomed to seeing those slimy, unprotected creatures inching their way across the green grass of their soggy existence. I also saw them obliterated because they had no protection in the world—very much like many of the partners of sexual addicts who reach out for help. One such woman told her group that her husband's addiction had obliterated her life and her *"self."* Although moving toward trust requires vulnerability, we can't afford to be like a slug. It's simply too risky and dangerous. How, then, should we approach it?

This brings us to sea turtles. Living under gloomy Seattle skies, famished for sunshine, my former husband and I spent most of our vacations during those years basking on warm beaches and enjoying the wonders of snorkeling. With snorkeling often comes sea turtles—those huge, gentle, inquisitive creatures that swim beside you in the warm sea.

Sea turtles are also vulnerable. Unlike land turtles, they cannot retract their heads and tuck them safely under their shells. In some parts of the world, people like to eat them. And both the increase in sea temperatures and the related stronger coastal storms endanger their existence. Sea turtles do, however, wear their own kind of protective boundary: a hard, bony shell. They cannot completely retract inside these shells, but neither are they totally exposed and vulnerable like the slug.

As you consider vulnerably working toward trust, remember the sea turtle. We can learn from them. Like the sea turtle's environment—beaches and oceans—the environment of marriage is also endangered. The *heating up* of our social environment by sexuality's pulsing surge is everywhere. No husband can avoid the daily onslaught of sexual stimulation, no matter how much he loves his wife and wants to remain mentally and physically faithful. Of course, this same environment also triggers our hurt, and we often respond by shutting down or getting angry. Our changing times do not provide a good environment for couples seeking monogamy and deep connection over the long haul of a shared life.

Yet like the sea turtle, we can develop a shell of protection. Though we can't fully tuck all the way under it while remaining present in our relationship, we can use the protective covering of detachment, boundaries, healthy self-talk, and healthy communication to provide a buffer between our tender tissue and the triggers that come at us.

As you consider vulnerably sharing your triggers, needs, and boundary requests, think of the sea turtle. Work at growing your protective covering, making sure it is composed of elements that will empower you to proactively share your needs, and to softly but assertively ask that they be met. In addition to boundary work, the little book, *Speaking Your Mind Without Stepping On Toes*, can help enormously with these much-needed skills.

At this point in your journey, which creature do you most resemble when it comes to your level of vulnerability? Are you in great risk of obliteration like the slug? Or do you already carry a protective shell of healthy detachment, healthy boundaries, and healthy communication skills, among other tools you've learned to wield? If you need to work at developing your protective covering, on which areas should you focus?

_____
_____
_____
_____
_____
_____
_____

## Things Your Husband Can do to Help Build Trust

There are some basic recovery-lifestyle changes that make true recovery from sexual addiction possible. Many appear on the following list. You may have others born out of what's occurred in your marriage. Use the lines at the bottom to add them.

A lifestyle of true recovery from sexual addiction includes:

- Establishing accountability with at least one other man.
- Building honest, emotional bonds with healthy men.
- Working with a therapist on family of origin issues and unresolved, emotional pain.
- Working a 12-Step sexual addiction recovery program.
- Changing TV viewing habits.
- Changing the kinds of movies watched.
- Changing the kind of books and magazines read.
- Safeguarding Internet usage.
- Maintaining honesty with you about temptations (but without detail and only if honesty helps you relax. Each woman has different needs in this area.)
- Offering reassurance that he is regularly taking steps to maintain sexual integrity.
- Sharing regularly with you about the women in his workplace.

- Calling to let you know if he's running late.
- Touching base during the day to provide assurance that you are on his mind.
- Responding with non-defensiveness and understanding when you need reassurance.
- _____
- _____
- _____
- _____
- _____
- _____
- _____

If you consistently saw your husband choosing to live his life in these ways, how might this help grow your trust?

_____
_____
_____
_____
_____
_____

What do you need to see in your husband to feel confident he has experienced true heart-change?

_____
_____
_____
_____
_____
_____

## Getting to Trust Is a Journey

Have an honest, open but loving talk with your husband about your desire to trust him. Let him know what he can do to help build that trust in you. Show him the above list. Don't be afraid to ask to have your needs met, using the skills you learned in the Boundaries Chapter. Trust requires great vulnerability on your part; and you've learned way too much to make yourself vulnerable again, without the one you love wanting to protect your heart as much as you do.

The responsibility is on him. You can take responsibility for appropriately meeting your own needs in many areas of your life, but this is not one of them. Rebuilding trust by changing the way he lives and talks is a concrete way your husband can work toward sexual sobriety and rebuilding his relationship with you.

Moral purity is difficult for husbands, but not impossible. If a man really wants purity, he will walk in accountability and remain in honest, accountable relationships with other men the rest of his life. He'll do that for his own good, as well as for the good of his marriage. Mental and physical sexual sobriety are possible.

Although *none* of us can know for certain what another human being is doing and thinking, we can relax and live life with joy as we see our husband striving for healthy change. No, we should never blindly trust a human being 100% because we are all human and therefore fallible. But we can live with peace if we see our husbands making these efforts. Even then, we'll need courage.

*Courage.* The word even sounds strong. Anchored. Brave. Dale Ryan explains courage for us:

> *Courage is not, of course, the absence of fear. It is not about being fearless. Courage is possible only when fear is still present. While we almost always prefer to respond to our fears by growing in our capacity for serenity, sometimes the only possible way to respond to our fear is by growing in our capacity for courage. And* **there is no faithlessness in being a person of courage.**[30] (emphasis added)

## Beginning Again

Change. Adaptation. Adjustment. These have by necessity become our new tasks. Only our faith can see us through. Faith alone can give us the courage to keep walking out this journey.

"Faith," wrote Tagore, the Indian poet, "is the bird that *feels* the light and sings while the dawn is still dark."

What role has faith played in your journey thus far? How might it help you in the future?

_____
_____
_____
_____
_____

---

[30] Dale Ryan, DMin (*The Fear Factor,* STEPS, volume 13, number 3, 2003), 3. Used by permission of STEPS and The National Association for Christian Recovery.

The months you've spent doing this workbook have provided a good beginning for your healing and growth. But in order to become healthier and stronger emotionally in the months ahead, you need to build ongoing growth into your life. This is important whether your marriage has survived or failed. If you plan to share your life with a man—your current husband or someone new—certain tools and skills will help you deal with the reality of the male mind as you now understand it.

Read books; work with groups or a counselor. Continue to expand your ability to use appropriate boundaries; to eliminate any codependency that may be veiled by your trauma; and to build your self-esteem. Leave your heart and mind open to forgiveness and trust. Work through any family of origin/childhood wounds, or other difficulties that may inhibit your freedom to be all God intends you to be. And remember this: men who struggle with sexual temptation also need to stay in accountability relationships and the recovery process for the rest of their lives. As long as we are on this earth, sexual temptation will not go away, and neither will the need to deal with it.

But no matter how hard we or our husbands work, we are a broken people living in a broken world. The agonizing, gut-wrenching truth is, there are no guarantees. No matter how hard you pray, you can't be certain your husband will never again give in to sexual temptation and betray his commitments. But if you want the chance to reconnect with him, or with any man in the future, you must take the risk love requires. C.S. Lewis said it best:

> "To love at all is to be vulnerable. Love anything and your heart will be wrung and possibly broken. If you want to make sure of keeping it intact you must give it to no one, not even an animal. Wrap it carefully round with hobbies and little luxuries; avoid all entanglements. Lock it up safe in the casket or coffin of your selfishness. But in that casket, safe, dark, motionless, airless, it will change. It will not be broken; it will become unbreakable, impenetrable, irredeemable. To love is to be vulnerable."
>
> — **C.S. Lewis, The Four Loves**[31]

As you walk through life, keep one hand in God's. He is, after all, the only One guaranteed worthy of your *complete* trust. He will *never* leave you if you make Him a part of your life.

## Finding Purpose in Your Loss

How has your life changed during the last few months?

_____
_____
_____
_____
_____

---

[31] C.S. Lewis, *The Four Loves* (New York, NY: Harcourt Brace, 1960).

Have there been any good things that have come with the changes? If so, what are they?

_____
_____
_____
_____

What new opportunities and choices would you like to explore?

_____
_____
_____
_____
_____

How do you feel when you think about your future?

_____
_____
_____
_____
_____

If you don't have a plan that will enable you to work toward the future you desire, consider enlisting a life coach. She can help you develop and work a plan that will give wings to your dreams and new meaning to your life. This may be one of the best investments in yourself you'll ever make.

As you look to the future, consider the nature of God, as reflected in this verse from the Old Testament book of Jeremiah:

> *"For I know the plans I have for you," declares the Lord, "plans to prosper you and not to harm you, plans to give you hope and a future."*
> —*Jeremiah 29:11*

May you know you are deeply loved by your Creator, and that He has a plan for your future. No matter what our losses, He still holds each one of us close as we live our lives one day at a time. I am asking Him for your continued healing and a heart filled with new joys in the months and years ahead.

Your sister on this journey,

*Marsha Means*, MA

## Tasks, Tools & Truths Discussed in this Chapter

1. Defining forgiveness: What it is, and what it is not.
2. Using the tool of reframing.
3. Forgiveness and the God Box.
4. Consider forgiving one thing at a time.
5. Trust must be earned by the addict.
6. Recovery behaviors that inspire trust.
7. Trust (and love) require vulnerability.
8. Finding for purpose in our pain is transformational.

## APPLICATION: APPLYING TRUTH TO LIFE

From my work in this section I realize that I need to take the following action steps:

_____
_____
_____
_____
_____
_____
_____
_____
_____
_____
_____

# Resources Available to You

## Free Phone Call

We are available to you for one no-cost, hour-long call. It's our gift for every new woman who comes our way, no strings attached, because we remember how desperately we needed support and direction when we were where you now find yourself. Simply fill out the assessment form on our website, www.acircleofjoy.com.

## Support Groups

- To help you heal from betrayal trauma: From Betrayal Trauma to Healing and Joy, a 12 week, telephone, small support group.
- Healing through Joy: 12-week group to learn more about how you can use the Life Model tools, i.e. intentional joy, increased capacity, and Immanuel moments, to take your healing further telephone, small support group.
- How to Set and Create Effective Boundaries: 12-week support group.

## Individual Coaching with One of Our Team Members

Marsha, Jodi, Katherine, Kristie, and Carin are available to you.

## Books for Your Healing

- *From Betrayal Trauma to Healing & Joy: A Workbook for Partners of Sex Addicts*
- *You Can Beat Anxiety Without Meds*
- *Your Sexually Addicted Spouse: How Partners Can Cope and Heal*
- *Real Hope, True Freedom: Understanding and Coping With Sex Addiction*
- *Healing Rain* – Devotionals for partners who've experienced betrayal trauma.

# Appendix A:

# How We Can Increase Our Capacity So We Can Heal

## The Pain Processing Pathway

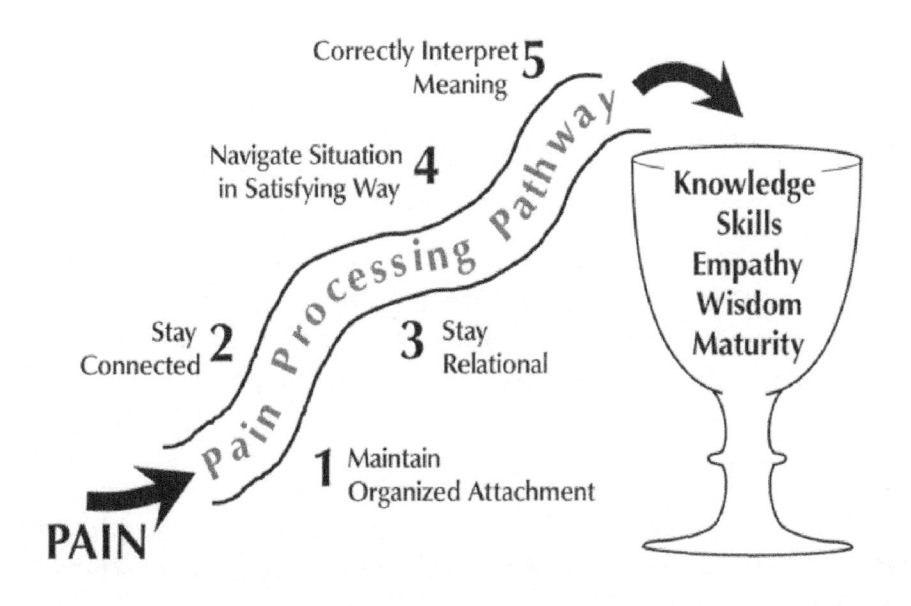

*Pain Processing Pathway*

PAIN → 1 Maintain Organized Attachment → 2 Stay Connected → 3 Stay Relational → 4 Navigate Situation in Satisfying Way → 5 Correctly Interpret Meaning → Knowledge, Skills, Empathy, Wisdom, Maturity

Let's look at each of the five components Karl Lehman, MD, tells us we need to do and use to heal trauma and integrate into our lives what we learned from that trauma.

## Organized Attachment

Looking at the list of five things we need in order to heal, number 1, organized attachment, is rooted in how we grew up and attachment theory. Having "organized attachment" requires that our parents did good parenting from our birth through the first several years of our lives. But few of us grow up that way, because life is full of surprises and hardships. And for those among us who grew up with a lot of trauma, gaining organized attachment will likely require some deep, one-on-one work with a therapist to heal old attachment wounds, if you haven't already done so. Because new trauma hooks old trauma, and the emotions we feel from both old and new get intermingled and tangled, old, unhealed trauma can make it hard to know what is causing our pain. And we missed out on great attaching from our parents, we need to heal and learn how to create attachments with those we care about in the present.

## Staying Connected

Staying connected is the opposite off isolating. It means *not* withdrawing and nursing our wounds. It means staying connected to the safe, supportive people in our lives; the people who have the capacity to walk with us through our pain. I see this work in my support groups where women make an effort to bond. Women connect via texting and chatting apps, and when they need support, they share and ask for it. I love that the same technology that has helped create the trauma in our lives can be put to work to help us heal. But the occasional group member who steps back from that connection, and usually isolates, is the one who doesn't heal. Learning to stay connected is required for healing, and also for healthy relationships.

## Staying Relational

Staying relational requires "keeping our relational circuits on". Dr. Lehman expands on that need below:

> *"We have been created to be relational beings—we have been created to be in relationship with God and with each other. Our minds and spirits have been created to desire relationship and to function best in relationship....When these brain circuits are functioning as designed, our spontaneous, normal experience will be to feel relationally connected and to feel the desire for connection.... Unfortunately, there are certain problems and conditions that can cause us to temporarily lose access to these brain circuits. When this happens, we operate in non-relational mode. Our spontaneous experience in non-relational mode will include the absence of feeling relationally connected, and we won't even want to be connected."*[32]

My personal and professional experience has taught me that when we are stranded in our pain and trauma, isolation can be a magnetic trap that pulls us in, making it difficult to reach out for help and support. Who among us hasn't wanted to lock the doors, draw the blinds, crawl in bed, and pull the covers over her head? In those times, our instincts for isolation become our worst enemy. Dr. Lehman is right: *we need each other to heal.*

That means that one way we can increase our capacity so we can heal is to stay connected and stay relational with those who truly care and understand, and who will walk with us as we heal.

---

[32] Karl Lehman, MD, *The Immanuel Approach for Emotional Healing & Life,* (Evanston, Il: Immanuel Publishing, 2016), 718-719.

**Navigating the Situation in a Satisfying Way** When
the insanity of sex addiction and the betrayal trauma it produces crash into your personal world, life as we thought we knew it is blown to pieces. The one we trusted our hearts to is suddenly a stranger, and both our past and our future are called into question. Healing from betrayal trauma requires a healing process, and a guide to lead us. If we can find and follow someone who has taken this journey before us, healed, and eventually landed on her feet, the trip will be shorter and the path to healing straighter, than if we are forced to try to heal alone. Gratefully, the last three decades have produced an over-abundance of available guides for this journey.

## Correctly Interpreting the Meaning of Our Pain

Like the concept above, correctly interpreting the meaning of our pain requires a guide. Without this help, our betrayal wound may scab over, and like an untreated wound, it won't heal. It will abscess and produce toxicity in the form of anger, shame, unforgiveness, a hardened heart, resentment, hate, or a mix of toxic emotions, that will eventually damage

# Appendix B:

# Understanding What It Means to be Male, Wounded & Addicted

"How could he do this to me? To our children? To God...and to himself?" Nearly all of us cry out these words in the early days of discovery that the men we gave our hearts and lives to have shattered our world by violating the sanctity of our marriages and giving away what we believed was only ours. Some have gone farther, violating legal boundaries and social norms.

Yes, how could he? How could they?

In the decades since I initially realized my need for answers to these painful questions, I've learned it is a rare man who wants to hurt his wife this way, and nearly every sex addict feels deep remorse and shame. And I've learned that inside nearly every grown-up sex addict hides a wounded little boy —a little boy who still feels the pain of long-ago emotional wounds because he has never found healing. And for most addicts, solid, *long-term* sexual sobriety remains slippery at best until someone helps that little boy-turned-grown-up-man shine a healing light on the ancient lesions in his psyche and soul. He must do the hard, slow work of tending these wounds.

Before we explore the reality fueling most sexual addiction, let's first confront a less troubling, though difficult, reality. Men are fundamentally different than women in at least three key ways that factor into the complexity of sexual addiction within our marriages.

## Lust Lurks Around the Edges of the Normal Male Mind

Honest men tell me the truth is, lust lurks just around the edges of the normal male mind. This potentially deadly challenge simply comes with being born male. Add a sexually charged society and Internet, and it often spells personal disaster. For most of us, this wasn't part of the fairy tale stories we heard growing up. And rarely is the issue discussed during premarital counseling.

Unprepared, we collide with this painful truth some time after the wedding night and it rips right through our hearts. Our dreams shatter, and we automatically think it's about us. We think we're simply not enough to keep our husbands from looking elsewhere. But the reality is, it has *nothing* to do with us. Many men struggling with lust are married to beautiful women they truly love. This temptation simply comes with being born male.

My brothers have a friend in ministry who is well into the later half of his life.

And he's blind. One day they asked him, "Tom, does being blind help with lust?"

"I wish I could say it did," Tom replied, "but that would be a lie."

Hmm . . . could it be this is a part of the curse—the result of human free-will choosing rebellion way back in the Garden of Eden—that now comes automatically with the package?

No one can explain this aspect of being male any better—or more honestly—than former Portland, Oregon minister, Bill Perkins, author of *When Good Men Are Tempted*. I hated this book when I first read it, because it made me face the truth. The first chapter is aptly named, "Why Naked Women Look So Good." Perkins says:

> *This chapter was birthed one Friday night while I was turning on my sprinkler system. As I walked across my yard I noticed that my neighbors' lights were on. Curious as to why they were up so late, I approached the fence and looked through the slats. I expected to see a handful of people playing cards inside their home. Instead I saw a beautiful young woman talking on the telephone. That wouldn't have been any big deal if she had been dressed. But she wasn't.*
>
> *Instantly my eyes locked on her. Adrenaline rushed through my body.*
>
> *After gazing at her for a few seconds, I pried myself from the fence. As I walked away, I wondered why a naked woman was so beautiful. And why would her beauty affect me that way.*
>
> *Since that experience fifteen years ago, I've addressed thousands of men and talked personally with others. I've administered confidential surveys to find out what men are really thinking and doing. In the process, I've discovered that every man has his own personal battle with lust. Nobody escapes its appeal. Nobody.*[33]

Not pretty, is it? But if we want to experience the joys that marriage potentially holds, it's a truth we must face, grieve, accept, and work with, even if we don't like it. Next, let's look at another basic difference between men and women.

## Men Don't Need Emotional Intimacy to be Sexual

Though difficult for most women to understand, men and women differ in their approach to the act of sex. Sexual addiction specialist, Dr. Milton Magness, explains:

---

[33] Bill Perkins, *When Good Men Are Tempted* (Grand Rapids, MI: Zondervan, 1997), 9.

> ...[W]omen and men approach sex differently. Women typically require an emotional connection with their partner if they are going to have sex. If problems or conflict exist in the relationship, they must be addressed before many women are willing to be sexual.
>
> It is a different story with men. Men don't have to have an emotional connection to have sex. They can completely separate sex from love or emotion. If a man wants to be sexual but there is some emotional baggage in the relationship, his wife will probably want to "unpack" that baggage before being sexual. If a man is not willing to wait or make the emotional investment in the relationship, he can masturbate—literally be sexual with himself and not have to expend any emotional energy.[34]

While we as women think of *making love*, men generally think of *having sex*. That difference really stings our hearts (and pride). Yet again, we only have so many choices, if deep, lifelong intimacy is what we seek. So this presents another fact we must face, grieve, accept, and adapt to if, like most women, our hearts long for a marriage partnership.

*But true intimacy is within a man's reach.*

The good news is, Perkins, Magness, and millions of others have learned to build healthy boundaries between their minds and the temptations they encounter daily as they move through life in a sexually saturated world. And they can grow, heal, and learn to tolerate their wives' needs and do the emotional work true intimacy requires. It can be done. It's hard work, and it has to be learned, practiced, and committed to daily, but it is possible.

And while it's hard for the man who's relatively undamaged by childhood pain, it poses a gargantuan feat for the huge percentage of those who harbor ancient, festered soul-wounds. Since the bulk of our spouses fall into that category, let's look more closely at what they face each day. Knowledge is power, and hopefully this knowledge will provide understanding that can lead us to empathy, especially if they desire to heal those painful memories. And if they don't? Well, it can enable us to realize we can't do it for them and to focus on helping and healing ourselves. We'll look more closely at those long-ago wounds in a minute, but first let's look at one more key difference between men and women.

## Men Are Like Waffles

The well-known book title, *Men Are Like Waffles, Women Are Like Spaghetti,* can help us understand the third key difference. Men tend to compartmentalize the areas of their lives, often keeping the compartments separate emotionally. Like the tiny squares on a waffle, each has little dams around it. But as women our minds look more like freshly cooked spaghetti—noodles intertwined and piled together on our plate. Our thoughts, emotions, and the many areas of our lives all wrap around each other. Everything connects.

---

[34] Milton Magness, DMin., *Hope & Freedom for Sexual Addicts and Their Partners* (Carefree, AZ: Gentle Path Press, 2009), 49, 50.

This recently became poignantly fresh for me when a client shared her husband's latest disclosure of sexual indiscretion:

> *And he said, "But Mary, it had nothing to do with you," she recounted then cried, "How could he say that? It has everything to do with me. I'm his wife!"*

He's like a waffle. In his mind, it's as if he'd used an eye dropper to drip syrup into one little square, being careful that none ran over into the squares of his marriage. Nice and tidy, they remained separate in his mind. Not so for Mary. Like most of us, Mary and her husband are—well, *married*—so to her *everything* is interconnected.

And we must adjust our thinking to accept yet another, uncomfortable reality.

## Addiction as Attachment Disorder

Embedded in the DNA of every human being lies a deep longing to form secure connections with others and share our heartaches and joys. Women and men need secure attachments, just as we need light, water, and the air we breathe. But the effects of sin—of human failure to parent and love well, and sometimes outright evil—have made secure relational attachments the exception rather than the norm. Even with "good enough" parents most of us grow up with at least minor attachment wounds that require work to heal.

Psychologists Tim Clinton and Gary Sibcy explain that ". . . an early attachment injury results when someone we love, someone who we think should love us, like a parent, fails to provide our fundamental safety and security needs. In the attachment bond, anything that stands in the way of our ability to access our support figure and threatens our sense of security—whether that threat is real or perceived—has the potential to cause an attachment injury. And such injuries can ignite life's core pains: anger, anxiety, fear, grief, and suffering of various kinds."[35]

## How Old Attachment Wounds Impair Our Ability to "Do" True Intimacy

From these important, early relationships, we develop our own *attachment style* which we instinctively use in our future relationships. If we didn't have a *secure* attachment with our early caregivers, we enter life with an automatic impairment in our ability to form healthy, secure attachments with others, even our marriage partners. In addition, we're left with an itch we cannot scratch and a hunger we cannot satisfy—something buried so deep we may not even be consciously aware of its presence. And even if we are, we can't figure out how to access it, or what it would take to make it go away. Like hunger, it gnaws; so we do many things to try to numb or medicate it. And as we seek to soothe, we become candidates for addiction, especially sexual addiction. Because sexual

---

[35] Tim Clinton, PhD, Gary Sibcy, PhD, *Attachments: Why You Love, Feel and Act the Way You Do* (Brentwood, NJ: Integrity Publishers, 2002), 36.

release stimulates the brain's pleasure center, the same part of the brain stimulated by cocaine and heroin, it provides a false sense of intimacy or attachment.

## How Pornography & Masturbation Fuel the Cycle

Psychologist Jim Wilder, a specialist in trauma and addiction, and founder of the Life Model, helps us better understand how two things often thought *normal* and *harmless* actually fuel this intimacy-disconnect. Because brain imaging reveals that the attachment/bonding center and the genital control are adjacent in the brain, Dr. Wilder believes the purpose of our sexuality is to synchronize emotional states and energy, as well as bond with another person.

"The problem with masturbation," Dr. Wilder explains, "is that it is synchronizing energy with nobody, and this leads a man to bond with himself, his fantasies, or other non-relational entities, which in turn leads a man to further isolation and compulsion."[36] Dr. Mark Laasar has coined this phenomenon, "false intimacy."

Experience with sexual addiction shows that orgasm bonds an individual with whomever or whatever the person is with, which also explains the myriad strange fetishes often present in sexual addiction. Clearly, pornography and masturbation feed our inability to "do" true intimacy and relationship. Considering these facts also helps us better understand the related problems referred to as sexual anorexia and emotional anorexia.

## Sexual Anorexia and/or Emotional Anorexia

### The Addiction Is Draining Sexual Energy

Pornography, masturbation, and all forms of sexual behavior outside of a bonded relationship often drain sexual and emotional energy away from the *coupleship*.

> One reason sexual addicts don't have sex as often with their spouses is because their acting out drains energy from the marriage.... Some sexual addicts are never sexual with other people but confine their acting out to viewing pornography, engaging in sexual cyber chat, or phone sex. And with all of these forms of behaviors, they usually masturbate . . . the goal of their sexual activities is not intercourse or sexual release; they are actually craving a neurochemical fix.[37]

### A Closer Look at How this Works in the Brain

Darrell Brazell, minister and recovering sexual addict, does a phenomenal job of simplifying extremely important, though complex, scientific data. This information is key to helping sexual addicts find lasting freedom and to helping us better understand

---

[36] Jim Wilder, PhD, quoted by Darrell Brazell in *Attachments*, a free download at www.newhope4si.com.
[37] Milton D. Magness, DMin, *Hope & Freedom for Sexual Addicts and Their Partners* (Carefree, AZ:Gentle Path, 2009) 46.

*From Betrayal Trauma to Healing & Joy*

what we're dealing with. The following transcription comes from "Brain Science of Sex and Addiction" a free MP3 download available on his website (**www.newhope4si.com**).

*PLEASE NOTE: While the brain is not this simple, Darrell's simplification places understanding and freedom within a layman's reach.*

"The brain is split into two sides. . . .The first thing you need to understand about the left-right split is that the left side of your brain is the file cabinet. It contains everything you know verbally and logically. The left side of your brain has a file folder for everything you know . . . but it's all verbal and logical.

"But the right side of your brain is experiential. When you think of your right side of your brain, think of experience. The right side of your brain remembers everything you have ever experienced. It is non-verbal, image-based, and focused on the voice tones rather than the verbal content. Therefore, while your left side has file folders for information, your right side has 3-D, high-tech Dolby surround sound, complete with emotions, touch, feelings, and even odors. . . . It's why people can have such a different response when I say the word, *dog*.

"If you grew up with your dog sleeping with you at night, and him being your best friend, you hear the word *dog*, and you have positive emotional and physical responses. You hear the word *dog*, and you feel good. If, however, you were attacked by a pit bull when you were three, you hear the word *dog* and a wave of uncontrollable fear flashes through your entire body. The right side of your brain is also the executive control center of your brain. This is critical, because it is important to understand that it is in charge. That's why [persons] who [have] been attacked by a pit bull as [children] can read all the information in the world about the positive effects of having a dog for a pet, and still be terrified at the mention of the word *dog*. They can't overcome their fear through verbal, logical explanations, but only by having new, positive experiences with friendly dogs. . . .

"It's also important to understand that the right side of the brain has a four-level, hierarchical structure . . . and it's dominant for emotions in the body. It notices, synchronizes, and remembers everything. That's why people sometimes have what's sometimes called *body memories* for things they can't consciously remember, but they can almost feel.

"Finally, the right hemisphere decides when the left hemisphere can change its beliefs. . . . What you need to know is that the left side of the brain doesn't like to change its mind. When you have information in those file folders, it believes that information is true, and it holds on to that, no matter how much evidence is put against it until the right side of the brain is disturbed enough with experience that it gives the left side of your brain permission to change. No amount of information in and of itself will make a difference until the right side of the brain is disturbed enough to tell the left side of the brain, 'It doesn't make sense; you have to come up with a new explanation.'

"Our brains work on a hierarchical structure. . . . In this five-level structure, nothing gets to Level Five without first passing through Levels One through Four. If there are problems in a foundational level, it doesn't matter what's in the upper levels. You are unable to act like yourself or function properly. The first level is what's called the Attachment Center. . . . This is (filled in by) the connections we had with our mothers and fathers in early childhood. And if this attachment is strong and secure, we have a strong foundation for life. However, if your family of origin was not healthy, and especially if you did not bond well, you will struggle with attachment pain that is the deep ache in your soul that you just can't quite put your finger on. It's sub-cortical, which means it's deeper in our brain than our conscious awareness. The pain, however, is the most excruciating pain known to man. And we do all sorts of crazy things to numb out attachment pain.

> "Level Two is our fear center; our amygdalae. You can picture them as two *guard shacks* in our brain that serve as interpreters and filters to determine whether things are going to be led through the brain. They interpret everything as good, bad, or scary. And if they read something as bad or scary, they shut down the gate and let nothing through. They shut down the upper part of our brain, and put us in survival mode. Nothing gets in, and our thoughts and actions get stuck in a survival loop that will do whatever is necessary to avoid pain and stay alive.
>
> Illustration 1: The amygdalae
> (from wikipedia.com)
>
> "Level Three is the Cingulate Cortex, our *identity center*. It's what allows us to be ourselves.

"Level Four is the control center of our brain. It is the part of our brain that has executive control over our cravings. For example, if you have a healthy prefrontal cortex, you're able to say *no* to the second piece of pie or the porn-spam email. If your prefrontal cortex is underdeveloped, or damaged through addiction, you have little or no impulse control.

"And Level Five is the left side of your brain, the informational file cabinet, that stores all verbal and logical information (which we discussed earlier). . . . The left side of your brain is the 'train's last stop,' and if the train gets derailed at any of the four previous levels, especially attachment pain and fear, *it doesn't matter what's in the left side.*

"The left side of your brain is powerless to make decisions when something goes wrong in Levels One through Four. If you have attachment pain or issues, which we all do, or if you are afraid, if you are terrified, guess what happens to all the information you have stuffed into the left side of your brain? It is inaccessible. That's why so much of what we try to do to stop sexual *sin* is powerless. . . .You can't get enough information to get out of your addiction. . . . All the information in the world is useless because it was inaccessible to me when my attachment pain and deep fears kick into overdrive.

. . . .

"What do you do to heal the brain? The first thing I must do is admit there has been great damage done to my physical brain. I must admit that things were missing in my past that should have built up the control center of my brain. I must admit that things were done to me, and things that I have done in my addiction have further damaged my brain. But secondly, I must arrest addictive behaviors. I must find a way to stop the acting out, because acting out continues to damage the very organ—my brain—that I'm trying to heal. . . . [But I] cannot successfully arrest addictive behaviors until I first begin addressing issues stored in the right side of their brain.

"So how do you do that? How do you address the right side of your brain? First and foremost, you heal the right side of your brain through relational connections with others. . . . Relational connections are the most powerful healing element to the right side of the brain. . . . The primary difference between guys who get healthy, and guys who don't is relational connections. . . . As long as it was just information they were merely stuffing more into the left side of their brain and they stayed stuck. On the other hand, we've had guys come (to our recovery group) who didn't do well in school, who struggled to read, do workbooks, etc, but they built relationships, they made daily phone calls, came to multiple groups each week, and while they continued to struggle, we could literally see them changing before our eyes. And as they grew stronger, they began to find freedom from their compulsive behaviors. . . . "

As Darrell discusses this further, he refers more to the attachment center and the role it plays in sobriety:

*This part of our brain is critical because it is the control center. . . .*

> *It is the part of our brain that has veto power over our cravings. . . . That part of our brain grows through relationships with others who are genuinely glad to be with us. God intends for it to grow primarily through the early childhood connections with our parents. However, the cool thing is . . . this part of the brain is capable of growth our entire lives. . . .*[38]

Very cool indeed, especially for the sexual addict who longs to break free.

## More on Healing Attachment Disorder

Dr. Phillip J. Flores, clinician and author of *Addiction as an Attachment Disorder*, writes about what it takes for addicted people with attachment wounds to fill the unfillable hole which began with a childhood attachment disorder. Addiction is obviously a deep attachment to a drug or a behavior; recovery is a deep, interdependent attachment to a new lifestyle and to people sharing that new lifestyle with us. Patients who have experienced severe and early childhood abuse and neglect will need intensive trauma therapy to heal those wounds, and they will also benefit greatly from structured group therapy, where they can learn to identify and express feelings in an honest, supportive environment.[39]

---

[38] Pastor Darrell Brazell, *Brain Science of Sex and Addiction*, a free download at www.newhope4si.com.
[39] http://www.caronrenaissance.org/media_center/|les/Attachment-DisorderCaronRenaissance.pdf Attachment.

Pastor Brazell shares this last thought on healing attachment disorder, which underscores Dr. Flores' writings:

> *Relational connection with others provides the most powerful healing to the right side of the brain, the "experiential" side, which is where healing must happen. Remember? The attachment center is behind the right eyeball. All the information in the world can only go into the left side of the brain, the "explaining" side. While learning about addiction can help educate, understanding how the entire brain works together is a key to helping people find long-term healing from addiction.*[40]

Dr. Jim Wilder and the clinicians with the Life Model, echo this finding from their clinical experience with thousands of wounded clients:

*They really need for the people who love them to encourage them to find out where their pain is coming from, and to accompany them on their path to recovery. Without the help of a caring community around them, their woundedness, dividedness, isolation, and oppression will prevent them from getting into wholeness.*[41]

If our situations—and the men we love—make it possible, Dr. Wilder's words provide wisdom for the caring, supportive role we may play for those who desire help and healing. But one additional, thorny issue presents in some sexual addicts, a fact we need to touch on.

## The Double Challenge of Dual Diagnosis

As if addiction and childhood wounds weren't enough to deal with, some sexual addicts suffer the additional struggle of a diagnosed mental illness. Others remain undiagnosed, uncertain why they struggle as they do. In clinical terms, those who suffer from mental illness *and* addiction are given the label, "dual diagnosed." In human terms, mental illness makes addiction more difficult to deal with because often the addiction arose as a mechanism to numb the person's original psychic pain. It probably won't surprise you that mental illness is often the byproduct of abuse in childhood, or what we've described as attachment wounds. If your husband has been diagnosed with bipolar disorder or some other mental health challenge, the task of knowing how to support (while using detachment to avoid enabling) requires that you seek outside support and guidance. For those who love persons with mental illnesses, I recommend regular attendance at weekly support group meetings. You need special support for this monumental challenge.

But before we begin to process the heavy information contained in this chapter, let's consider, in general, what we can do to support our husbands.

---

[40] Darrell Brazell, *Brain Science of Sex and Addiction*, a free download at www.newhope4si.com.
[41] Shepherd's House, Inc, *Living From the Heart Jesus Gave You* ( Pasadena, CA: lifemodel.org), 21.

## So What Can We Do?

In addition to the many things we've learned and worked on in earlier chapters, what can we do besides come to terms with these hard realities? Our answers to that question will vary, depending on each husband's story and his response to personal failures and brokenness.

Some among us will have no choice but to accept a husband's decision to spurn his marriage vows and continue in addiction, leaving us with the hardest of choices to make: the possibility of leaving the marriage. A few of us will be blessed with remorseful husbands who actively seek the best help for healing themselves and restoring their marriages.

But most of us will be required to take a *tough love* position before the men we love will reach out for help. Your own tough love stance may have already paid off in rewarding dividends. Or, you may still be waiting and hoping for the miracle that could open the door to the healing of your marriage. On the other hand, you may not yet know what tough love looks like. Since most of us must play the "Tough Love Card" as we face this pain, let's talk about what tough love looks like.

## Just What Is Tough Love?

*Love Must Be Tough*[42] by Dr. James Dobson remains a staple in helping us learn to be "wise as serpents, yet gentle as doves" when tough love is required. Tough love entails the skills of detaching, self-soothing to stay calm in the face of chaos, and accessing our impersonal energy for strength, all things we talked about in earlier chapters. It also requires confrontation and firm, loving boundaries that require admission, seeking help, and true change.

Tough love is not hate; nor is it faithlessness. Even as our exceedingly loving but righteous God imposes consequences—consequences as far reaching as eternal separation from Him—so, too, are we required to love toughly under our present circumstances. For most women, this task is not only confusing and exceedingly difficult, it is also heart-rendingly painful. Tough love requires true commitment—a commitment of seeking to imitate God's love, even when it requires imposing consequences.

Most of us choose the less godly path of passivity; yet even in our lack of overt action, the bitter bile of resentment slowly eats away at our hearts and the heart of our love for the addicts in our lives. Tough love requires we respect our husbands enough to impose godly consequences, doing our painful part to help them become the men God created them to be from the moment each one was conceived. If we want to fight for our marriages, we must learn to love toughly.

---

[42] James Dobson, PhD, *Love Must Be Tough* (Nashville: Thomas Nelson: 1996.)

## Partnering with the Potter

The Life Model highlights our "true identity"—that aspect of our nature which God created us to fully become. However, *becoming* is a process. Sometimes it's a painful process, and certainly one that requires hard work, risks, and learning new ways to think and feel and grow, none of which can happen without the risk and work of building new, life-giving relationships where all this can take place.

But when an addict is using any number of game plays to break through your tough love, it's hard to remain loving, detached, calm, and consistent. And it's especially difficult to remain strong and consistent when the thing we require proves extremely challenging for him to do, which might include the following:

- Does he need inpatient treatment to heal?
- Does he need to draw temporary boundaries between himself and his emotionally unhealthy family members who topple his efforts to grow?
- Does he need to learn to take responsibility financially in his efforts to grow and be sober in all areas?
- Does sobriety require he let go of a high stress job he loves in order to beat his addiction?

This is the world we live in when we love a sexual addict: a world riddled with risks and unpleasant possibilities. Understanding his struggle, you can partner with him by expressing "tough love with purpose," encouraging him to chip away the layers that hide the true man. This task is anything but easy. But if you love him, and if he is willing, he *can* become the unique and gifted man his Creator fashioned him to be. He *can* gain freedom from his sexual addiction.

How do you feel knowing that struggling with sexual temptation and lust might require your husband to walk in accountability and commitment to mental monogamy for the rest of his life? It might mean the weekly SA meetings won't cease this side of heaven. Does this make you sad, or does it give you hope? Why?

_____

_____

_____

_____

_____

What have you lost in relation to these two key differences between men and women: (1) men don't need emotional intimacy to be sexual, and (2) men are like waffles?

_____
_____
_____
_____
_____

Does knowing about these differences make you feel vulnerable to future hurt? Why or why not?

_____
_____
_____
_____
_____

Do you think you can ever trust your husband, knowing his struggles with sexual addiction? Why or why not?

_____
_____
_____
_____
_____

How have you changed in response to this pool of information?

_____
_____
_____
_____

Does this knowledge color your view of men in general? If so, how do you feel about their struggles and issues with sexual temptations?

_____
_____
_____
_____
_____

To your knowledge, does your husband carry attachment wounds that remain unhealed? If so, how might you offer support and encouragement in the hope he will find help to heal them?

_____
_____
_____
_____
_____

If your husband is truly working toward sexual sobriety, what can you do to "let go and let God" give you peace and be your anchor as you share your life with a man who is taking responsibility for his sexual purity with openness and consistency?

_____
_____
_____
_____
_____

You cannot be your husband's accountability partner. That role needs to be filled by another man who are working hard to maintain his own sexual purity. But you can have a relationship filled with mutual respect, honesty, and reassurance. That *safety* will encourage his open and honest communication. Yet only you know what you can and cannot do to support your husband, while still taking care of yourself. Find a healthy balance in your relationship that honors both of you during his initial recovery process.

How do you feel about being a safe person for your husband? What feelings emerge as you consider this?

_____
_____
_____
_____
_____

*From Betrayal Trauma to Healing & Joy*

## In Case You Want to Know: More From Dr. Milton Magness...

### *Why Does He Lie Even When He Doesn't Need To?*

"Will you ever be able to trust your partner again?...You want to trust the person you love, but you have found that there is a web of deception between the two of you and you wonder if your partner will ever be truthful with you.

. . . An addict lies not only to cover up acting out, but to preserve the image of himself that the unsuspecting spouse or partner has. Sexual addicts believe that if their partners knew everything they had done in the past as well as their current acting-out behaviors, they would not stay in the relationship.

. . . Lying may be the toughest habit for your spouse or partner to break. For some sexual addicts, even after they have stopped acting out and have started doing significant work in recovery, they find lying to be a habit that is difficult to sever.

. . . Initially, lying may be a survival skill. If a child has a parent who is abusive and perhaps even caught up in his or her own addiction, a child may lie to keep from being abused. Or if a child is neglected, ignored, or in some other way marginalized, he or she may lie to get attention. Sometimes children with learning disabilities or other limiting factor may lie to appear more normal."

## Couple's Intensives with Dr. Magness

Dr. Milton Magness is without a doubt the very best investment I know of to help a couple save and heal their marriage damaged by sexual addiction. He does three-day intensives with individual couples. We've seen scores of couples utilize this resource and go on to not only heal, but to thrive. The percentages are astounding. You can learn more about these powerful intensives at his website: **www.hopeandfreedom.com**.

## Additional Outstanding Resources

Daniel Amen, M.D. (**www.brainplace.com**): Renowned neuropsychiatrist with catalog of over 50,000 SPECT scans of brains, including sexually-addicted brains, showing the damage addiction does to the brain's organic structure.

Dr. Allan Schore (**www.allanschore.com**): Often referred to as the Einstein of psychiatry.

What in this chapter is hardest for you to accept?

## APPLICATION: APPLYING TRUTH TO LIFE

From my work in this section, I realize I need to . . .

# Appendix C:

# When Your Marriage Fails

I've never met a woman who, on her wedding day, walked down the aisle, hoping that one day she would be divorced. Virtually every bride on the planet who is allowed to make her own choice is certain her marriage will be different because she and her soon-to-be-husband share a love unlike any other. Theirs is deeper, wider, richer, and stronger than the ordinary love other couples feel. *Theirs* will stand the test of trials and time.

Yet the divorce statistics—and real life—reveal a different story. About half of all marriages are destined for failure, and nothing places greater strain on love and marriage than sex addiction and the searing pain of betrayal trauma. Virtually every woman who discovers her husband's secret life wonders, *Is this the end of 'us'?* Marriage—especially in the digital age—is more than hard work. It can be excruciatingly painful because nearly all of us truly love our husband. And for those of us who lose our marriages? It breaks our hearts to leave what we thought would last a lifetime.

The good news is that if an addict is willing to do the hard work required to beat his addiction and to deal with the habits of lying, gaslighting, and hiding emotionally, most wives can eventually heal and recommit. But sadly, not all sex addicts have access to help that can enable them to stop the emotional hiding, and others aren't willing to do the hard, life-changing work required to beat this addiction. And when they aren't, their partner faces an agonizing choice: do I stay, or do I file for a legal separation or divorce?

There is no one-size-fits-all answer to those questions. Every marriage and family presents a unique constellation of individuals, challenges, lifestyles, and needs, so each requires a unique deliberation. And unless there is other abuse, it's important not to make a hasty and final decision; it takes time to find your own "right" choice.

If you are contemplating divorce, my assumption is that you've already tried hard to save your marriage and family. You've confronted; you've told him this is a deal-breaker; you've sought marriage counseling, dragging him with you. And you've asked that he get into sex addiction recovery and attend 12 step meetings, find and work with a sponsor, and asked him to work with a therapist on childhood issues. Some husbands will do all these, and gain freedom from their addiction. Others will do them, and still fail to stay "sober." And others still will ignore their partner's requests for recovery work, making it clear they don't plan on changing.

If you fall into that last category, you are likely ready to move into the pre-planning phase of ending your marriage. If that's where you now find yourself, don't rush to the courthouse and fill out paperwork. Ending a marriage and family is serious business, and the first phase requires critically examining multiple areas of your life, so you make the right choice for you and your family.

And it's imperative you are ready financially before you tell your husband you are done. The one exception is marriages marred by domestic violence. If you or your children are being abused or are in other danger, you *must* protect your children and yourself, even if you aren't ready. To do otherwise is to risk losing custody when Child Protective Services somehow finds out you kept your children in a toxic, violent situation. If your marriage includes abuse, seek guidance from a local women's shelter. They can also put you in touch with an attorney, who will likely provide some legal guidance for free, or at a deep discount. I've had wonderful mothers lose permanent custody of their children, so please, please take this warning seriously.

## Phase 1: Determine Your Unique Circumstances

A long list of questions must be answered before you make any life changes. Use this phase to gather information, so you can make a truly informed decision about your future. Every woman's situation is unique, so think in terms of your unique circumstances as you begin to answer these questions, then use your answers to create a plan that fits you and your family.

After this phase, some women decide it's best if they stay in their marriages, at least for now. And others make that decision permanent, finding other ways to cope with their circumstances. Near the end of this appendix, I've shared one woman's story about how she came to that decision. But for now, let's look at your unique circumstances.

1. Do you have a circle of trustworthy support, made up of people who will be there, even after you file for divorce? If not, work to build it. Adequate support is crucial. Life will be so much easier if you have support in place.

2. Are you physically well and able to work? If you still have young children, can you make peace with being away from your children while you work? If you can't make peace with it, would it be better to wait until the children are older? Find the right answer for you, perhaps talking to other single mothers who've made the decision to leave.

3. How old are your children, and what are their needs? Do you have a child with special needs? What are their needs over the next 10 – 15 years? College tuition? An extra vehicle

so older children have transportation for work? Your children's needs will be unique, so consider them carefully, *before* making your final determination.

4. Can you support yourself and any minor children? If not, what will it take to become financially independent? Do you need training, or some time back in school to brush up on your skills? Get career guidance, and based on what you learn, develop a plan for financial freedom. Some men play hard-ball once the divorce begins, so financial independence is crucial. It gives you the ability to keep your "ship" afloat, even if he tries to sink it by withholding money.

5. What about health insurance? The children will likely be covered by their father's health insurance, providing he has it. But you will need insurance too, so consider this expense as you pre-plan. While some jobs provide coverage, others do not, so plan wisely.

6. Where will you live? If you have minor children, child custody laws in your state will dictate whether or not you can move out of the state. In addition, if you and your husband have been buying your home, leaving the family home prior to a divorce settlement can cut into your rights as a co-owner. This is an area where you must get legal guidance. Otherwise, you could lose your rights to your home.

7. Do you have access to all financial and legal records? Sadly, some sex addicts move funds, block their wife's access to at least some accounts, or make sure her name is not on property titles. If you learn your husband has done any of these, please buy and read, *High-Conflict Divorce for Women,* by Debra Doak, and/or *The Complete Guide to Protecting Your Financial Security When Getting a Divorce.*

No doubt you will think of other questions you need to answer before you are truly ready to take action. Allow some time to pass while your brain sorts through the files of your life. Otherwise, you might miss important details pertinent to your circumstances.

## Spend Time Gaining Clarity in Each Category

As you think through each of the seven categories above, you will no doubt see areas where you need to strengthen your hand before you make a move. If you need to build a stronger circle of support, invest in growing authentic relationships. You might do that in a faith-based community; your recovery community; a club you belong to; or volunteering for a good cause.

But the two categories that will require the biggest time investment are finances and your work life. Let's look at finances first, because finances will dictate your possible need to reenter the workforce.

*From Betrayal Trauma to Healing & Joy*

## Gaining Clarity and Documentation of Your Household Finances

1. Before you can make an informed decision to leave your marriage, you need a clear picture of where you and your spouse stand financially. Even if your husband has been fair with finances, this category is essential. You need copies of at least the last three years' taxes, all mortgages, loans, bank accounts, credit card accounts, insurance policies, retirement accounts, and anything else related to finances.

   Determine what you own, as well as what you owe. Determine all assets and their current value. And determine all household income, remembering to document everything. This may be impossible if your husband is self-employed and has made it difficult to trace finances. A few clients have had to use forensic accountants to access actual earnings. Also, look up your credit score as a couple.

   Make digital (if not paper) copies and save them on duplicate flash drives. Then put one in a safety deposit box at a different bank than the one you and your husband have used. And keep the other flash drive in a secure location where you can readily access it.

2. Open a bank account in your name at the bank where you keep the backup flash drive and begin contributing to it regularly. You may only be able to deposit small amounts, but do it consistently. If you decide to stay in your marriage, taking these steps will help you take more responsibility for your life and your happiness. And in a compromised marriage, the ability to take responsibility for yourself is a strong benefit. Until his heart softens and he chooses strong recovery, it falls to you to take care of yourself.

3. Get a credit card in your name only, and use it to begin to build your own credit score. Nerdwallet.com is one place that can help you get started. Once you have a credit card in your name, use it regularly, but you must pay off the entire balance every month for the sake of your credit score, so only use it to the level that you can pay it off. This will help you establish a good credit score, which, trust me, is a girl's best friend.

## Confronting the Strong Possibility You Will Have To Work

Alimony is not guaranteed these days, and when it is awarded, it's usually not enough to live on, even when paired with child support. And both are likely to end in due time.

But do you have health challenges that make it extremely difficult to work? Do you have a child with special needs? What are your children's needs over the years until they launch out on their own? Who is going to pay for their college tuition? Can you count on your husband to meet his financial obligations after the divorce? Often, a formerly nice man begins to play dirty during the divorce process. One of the most painful parts of my work is watching some divorced mothers struggle because their former husbands seem to delight in making their lives hard and painful.

If you still have young children, you may not have a good option. If your marriage is toxic because of your husband's choices, keeping kids in that environment can damage them. But if you leave and have to work, there will likely be other losses. So moms with young children must think through their situation and decide if it might it be better to wait until they are older. There is no one-size-fits-all solution with young children.

In addition, pre-think childcare before you act, since it's not only expensive, it's hard to trust a stranger with our children.

If you aren't currently active in your own career, I strongly recommend you seek career guidance and testing. Find out where your gifts lie, if you don't have a strong career-path interest. And seek guidance in both the time and financial investments required for a variety of career paths. If you have a degree, but time has passed since you used it, find out what is needed to bring your skills up to speed. Do Internet research using terms like 'women's career guidance centers' in your town, or the nearest city. Community college counselors may also be able to help.

Once you complete all the steps in Phase 1, you will be much better prepared to make a decision. If you are leaning toward leaving your marriage, it's time to move into Phase 2.

**Phase 2: Planning for the divorce**

If, after investing time and soul-searching, you determine divorce is the only way to save your emotional and mental health, and financially you can afford to leave the marriage, you have entered Phase 2 of the process. It's time to revisit the areas in Phase1, plus any additional items you've added, and to create an action plan for each area. Divorce creates upheaval in your life, in your children's lives, and brings change to the larger family system. There is no such thing as an easy divorce, but preparation can help you and your children survive the painful life-quake a divorce almost always creates.

## Emotional Support

Hopefully you've invested in strong relationships as you've considered the option of leaving your marriage. Deep friendships require time and mutual contribution, so this is an area of planning that can't be put off until right before you file. But it is time spent wisely that will pay off in rich rewards down the road. It helps enormously to know you are not alone.

## Location, Location, Location

Where will you live? Women often assume they can go "home" in the event of a divorce, so they will have family support and childcare. But virtually all have faced the bitter disappointment of legal restraints around custody and visitation. Generally, the kids must stay near their dad, and time must be split with him. So legal advice early in this process is essential as you plan.

### *Leaving the Home Could Affect the Interest you Have in the Property*

If you and your husband have been buying your home, you *must* get legal advice before leaving the family home prior to the divorce settlement, so you know your state's laws about your rights to your home. If the marital situation becomes too stressful, and you feel desperate to move out, try to continue to pay a portion of the mortgage each month, and document them.

If there is abuse, document, document, document. Abuse is difficult to prove unless ER and other medical records back up your claims. In lieu of medical documentation, eyewitnesses can be helpful, if people are willing to take that on. If there is abuse and you are unable to get an order of temporary possession, it's imperative to take whatever steps you need to protect yourself. Leave the home if you feel you are in danger. But if there is a history of domestic violence, discuss it with your attorney because he or she may be able to legally have your spouse removed from the marital home.

### *Leaving the Home Could Affect Your Kids' School*

If you want your children to continue attending the same schools so friendships and activities aren't disrupted, you will likely need to stay in the same school district. If staying in the home is an option, do so, at least for a while, to keep the children's lives stable (home, school, friendships, extracurricular activities). Divorce is hard enough for children, without a passel of other simultaneous changes. If you can't afford to stay in the home, but your spouse's income is greater than yours, your attorney may seek to negotiate how much of the mortgage your husband will pay, to keep the children's lives more stable. Courts often rule in the children's favor.

### Finances and Work

### *Prepare an After-Divorce Budget*

It's time to determine how much money you will need to cover living expenses once you are divorced. Of course, your income determines much of your budget, as does your divorce settlement. So at this stage, create a barebones budget, based on essentials. That gives you a starting point as you plan. This will guide you as you seek employment, and your attorney negotiates the divorce settlement.

### Evaluate and Protect Financial Accounts

It isn't uncommon, after learning there is an impending divorce, for a spouse to raid financial accounts. Sometimes it's done in anger, sometimes it's done on the advice of an adversarial attorney. That's why pre-planning and documentation are so important *before* your husband knows about your plan to file for legal separation or divorce.

## Follow Your Attorney's Advice Regarding Credit Accounts Once You File

Contact and alert creditors to the fact that you are going through a divorce. If there is a change of address, make sure they have it so that you will continue to receive bills from all joint accounts that remain open. Your attorney will guide you on what to do about credit card accounts. But make sure all credit card bills are being paid. Divorce proceedings can take months and all it takes is one late payment to hurt your credit. Even if you have to pay the minimum on accounts that you know will ultimately be your spouse's responsibility, your credit score will be worth it.

If it's an amicable divorce, it will be easier and less expensive if you and your spouse are able to settle without litigation. But if it can't be done, make sure you have an attorney who is capable and willing to litigate your case before a judge. In this situation, you are basically looking for two things: an attorney who knows the value of settling quickly, but who is also willing to fight for you, should the need arise.

Don't spend the money foolishly, and document every penny you spend. Your records will help during settlement negotiations or in court.

## Health insurance

Unfortunately, at this writing, the United States still doesn't have universal health care. But healthcare for your children is essential, so check to make sure they will continue to be covered under their father's health insurance, assuming he has it. But also pay attention to health insurance benefits as you seek employment. Nothing breaks us faster than a dire diagnosis and hundreds of thousands of dollars in hospital bills. Even if you are young, consider health insurance absolutely essential, and find a way to get it. The stress of betrayal trauma so often ignites widespread inflammation in our bodies, and inflammation creates a vast array of other health issues, many of them serious. So find a way to get health insurance.

## Proximity to Care for Any Special Needs

If you are required to leave your family home, precheck possible new locations to be sure that any special medical (or other) needs will be readily available to you or your children in your new location. Driving long distances to special appointments, especially in winter weather, can be costly in time, money, and risk.

## Be on Your Best Behavior

Some people will automatically judge you for filing for divorce, and more than likely some will gossip. So be careful not to give anyone anything to gossip about. And be aware details of your life can end up in a divorce courtroom. Make your reputation and your parenting your highest priorities, along with nurturing supportive female relationships.

For the children's sake, it is important that whoever decides to leave the marriage is able to do so in a civil and respectful manner. I've seen a woman's deep depression and anger be used against her in a courtroom, so work for emotional stability. If you need medication to be stable, don't be afraid to ask a doctor for help.

The decision to divorce is usually very painful. You need to know that your decision will have a lasting impact on you, your children, and their father for the rest of your lives. So take your time and be sure it's the best option for you. To help you find your own best answer, below I share two women's stories. One from a woman who chose to stay, and the other woman who eventually left.

## One Woman's Story: Why I Chose to Stay

Two questions helped me as I considered the possibility of divorce. They were:

1. What can I *not* live with? This question forces us to determine our "deal-breakers." These are the behaviors we know we cannot and will not tolerate in our marriage. When we encounter true deal-breakers, the choice to stay is no longer an option, at least not long term. But sometimes leaving takes time. It can require time to plan and prepare, even if we don't want it to. However, having a plan, and persistently working it, will enable us to leave as soon as the pieces of our plan are in place.

2. What can I live with? Most of us at least consider leaving. And when we do, we're forced to examine our ability—or inability—to make it on our own, if we leave the marriage. Finances, children, family matters, or health issues might make staying the wisest—or the only—choice. At least for a season. I took the time I needed to sift through all of the painful feelings of betrayal, abandonment, loss, and feeling less-than, and eventually, I chose to stay, even though my marriage wasn't healed.

These two questions helped me gain the clarity and peace I needed to make healthy decisions about my life and my future. You may have different questions you need to answer, because each of our journeys is uniquely our own.

## Coming to Understand the Strange World Of Sex Addiction

At some point post-discovery, our shock wears off, and we try to learn what sex addiction, and how to care for ourselves in a marriage tainted by it. Like me, many partners realize, for their own reasons, they need or want to stay in their marriage. Some women will stay for a short while as they work their plan and prepare to leave. And others will choose to stay, perhaps permanently. Either way, partners can use this time to learn, heal, and prepare for their future.

## Six Tasks that Equip Us to Heal Whether We Choose to Stay or Leave

The following task list helped me take responsibility for my own well-being, and it kept me from slipping into the negative patterns that can come when married to a sex addict.

### Finding Support

Support and a healing process is crucial for partners of sex addicts. One of the best resources available is, *From Betrayal Trauma to Healing and Joy* workbook. Working through this workbook with a coach and a small group of women is the best gift you can give yourself. At the end of the 12 weeks, you will have been given the opportunity to share your story in a safe setting while gaining new skills and tools to use not only in your marriage but in every relationship in your life.

### Separating Your Healing from the Addict's

After I learned as much as I needed to about this addiction, I focused my energy on learning ways to heal from my trauma symptoms. And I learned that if we want to heal, we must separate our healing from that of the sex addict. Learning how to detach and refocus on our own healing for a season is one of the hardest things we must do, but without it, we will never heal.

### Utilizing the Power of the Serenity Prayer

The Serenity Prayer can bring calm, clarity, and peace in the space of thirty seconds. It's like a form of spiritual breathing. The simplicity of this prayer helps me discern my needs and helps me access the empowerment I need to meet them. It enables me to "let go" when needed, and it provides a continuing source of courage and comfort. I love its wisdom and its simplicity: *God grant me the serenity to accept the things I cannot change, the courage to change the things I can, and the wisdom to know the difference.*

### Learning and Using Boundaries

Learning how to detach from my husband in a healthy way provided a safe space to learn and create the boundaries I needed to begin to heal. It took a lot of trial and error, but I eventually learned how to create healthy boundaries to keep myself safe. If you need help with boundaries, Coach Carin facilitates a boundaries support group for that purpose[1].

---

[1] Carin Dusse, MA ; www.BetrayalTraumatoHealingandJoy.com.

## Taking Responsibility for Our Own Well Being

The Life Model has played an important role in my healing. And nothing is more powerful in helping us take responsibility for our own healing and well-being than the Life Model principles. Learning to "return to joy from negative emotions," and "using joy to increase my emotional capacity so it's higher than my pain" were foundations for me. Another Life Model principle that's helped me is "Learning to suffer well." This means, "Can I be true to who I am in the midst of suffering?" We touch on the Life Model principles in our From Betrayal Trauma to Healing & Joy groups, but if you want to learn more about these concepts and skills, consider participating in a Healing through Joy group once you've finished Betrayal Trauma to Healing & Joy.

## Finding Purpose in Our Pain

While early post-discovery is a very painful time, finding "the purpose in the pain" is highly valuable. Women have even said it is a sacred time where they feel more connected to their true self. Once they experience "being well," and learn new ways to take care of themselves (or return to activities that bring them joy), wonderful, beautiful things can happen. And they learn how to be well in a less than ideal marriage.

In time, I was able to regain a sense of safety and security, even though my marriage wasn't healed. Now, more than ten years post-discovery, I see myself in a different place. I still have triggers, but they no longer have the power to hijack my brain. I can access and use empowerment to take care of myself in healthy ways. And I know I can leave if I am not able to keep myself emotionally, psychologically, spiritually, and physically safe while staying married.

I encourage you to find the resources and tools you need to heal, whether or not your husband chooses recovery, and whether or not you stay. Healing is possible for any woman who discovers she is married to a sex addict.

While I did not choose this addiction, I do get to choose my story. I am not responsible for my husband's recovery, but I am responsible to make sure this addiction doesn't get "two for the price of one." Ten years ago I was determined to find the help and support I needed to heal and feel like myself again, and I'm so glad I did. My hope is that you will find the help you need to heal from the pain this addiction has brought into your life.

# The Story of a Woman Who Left

## Is My Life a Failure?

Someone told me my life as a wife of a sex addict is not a success story. It's really a story of failure. Bless this woman. She was speaking her truth during a support group I was facilitating. To her, success was a marriage that was healing and succeeding after sex addiction. And sadly, mine did not.

Most women who come to me as a coach want to hear success stories. Stories of marriages that faced the odds and healed from the relational betrayal this addiction brings. And that's the story I wanted to have; a story that spoke of how my husband battled this addiction and won after 50+ years. That he became all that I knew he could be. A man of integrity, a faithful husband, and an involved and present dad to our kids. That for us, true intimacy was growing, and we were being used powerfully to speak into the lives of others who struggle with sex addiction and intimacy anorexia.

But my story didn't turn out that way.

For six years, my husband did succeed in overcoming his addiction. But unfortunately, he never chose to get the help he needed to deal with the many areas of hurt and brokenness in his life. Nor did he do anything to deal with the 18 years of intimacy anorexia. Instead, he chose to ignore that unbelievably painful element I lived with. For you wives who have lived this, I know you understand. Yes, he had stopped looking at porn, but in every other area, there was no progress.

Then, after six years of being free, he chose to go back to his addiction. That, my sisters, is the story of my marriage.

But honestly, I don't see my life as a failure because my marriage came to an end. I treasured my marriage. I thought I would be married to my best friend forever. You don't give up easily on a marriage you've worked so hard to heal. I took a whole lot of time seeking God on this. My marriage didn't fail because I didn't pray hard enough for my husband, our marriage, and our children, because I did.

To walk away was one of the most difficult decisions I had to make. I cared deeply for my husband; and I still do. But my divorce doesn't define me. We are still friends. And we have family time during the holidays and birthdays. I still pray for him, and I still care deeply about him and his well-being.

God didn't fail me. He has been faithful throughout this journey. Today, I am thankful for this journey. I have found peace and contentment, and my capacity for joy has grown significantly. I thank God for what I've gone through because it has led me here where I coach amazing, courageous women from all around the world. I love how God has redeemed my life. I would not be doing this work if I hadn't walked this very difficult journey.

So is my life a failure?

Well, I'll leave that answer to those who really know me. But I know how God answers this question because He's told me.

Printed in Great Britain
by Amazon